selected poems 1968 - 2022

Selected Poems 1968 - 2022

Larry Kimmel

café nietzsche press
windsor, ct

selected poems 1968 - 2022

café nietzsche press
an imprint of:
bottle rockets press
p.o. box 189
windsor, ct 06095
www.bottlerocketspress.com
bottlerockets_99@yahoo.com

see also:
https://larry-kimmel.com

364 Wilson Hill Road
Colrain, MA 01340
https://larry-kimmel.com
starkmtpress@gmail.com

Image from Pixabay
Cover Design: Larry Kimmel

Printed in the United States of America 2021

ISBN: 979-8-9892491-5-2

For those who have underwritten my years,
gone the distance, kept the faith.

————————

"Ah, but a man's reach should exceed his grasp,
Or what's a heaven for?"

Andrea del Sarto
Robert Browning

"I regret little, I would change still less."

Andrea del Sarto
Robert Browning

PART ONE

TAKING NOTICE
from: **Unworldly Wind**

I Step Out on My Porch Near Midnight 1

Feeding Chickadees in Winter 2

Branch after Branch 3

Crossing the Connecticut River 4

The Winter Woods 5

Spring Beauties 6

An Easter Morning 7

Taking Notice after a Long Dark Night 8

Maple Keys 9

Jack-in-the-pulpit 10

E.H. Shepard's Painting of Eeyore's Birthday 11

After Reading an Epic Fantasy 12

Paths that Crossed 13

The Weight of One Small Death 14

View from a North Window 15

Each Stone 16

November Gold 17

from:

A RIVER YEARS FROM HERE

There is a River Years From Here 21

The Latch 22

Steel Town 23

Eleven to Seven 24

The Sliver of Steel 25

Member of the Club 26

Consider the Inch-worm 27

Black Ant Experiment 28

The Wasp & The Spider 29

On the Verge of Autumn 30

And Other Important Things..................................... 31

Evening Walk 32

Japanese Lanterns 34

Tidings 35

The Putting Away of Rookie 36

Star 40

THE JOHNSTOWN FLOOD
from: **Unworldly Wind**

The Johnstown Flood .... 43 - 48

THE WINTER OWL

The Winter Owl .... 51 - 59

A CUP FOR ALL SEASONS
from: **Unworldly Wind**

A Cup Full of Seasons 63
Posterity 66
Catnip Tea 67
Home of the Brave 68
In Memoriam 69
Wooden Chain 70
The Class Ring 71
October Elegy... 72
Regret 74

SEEKING THE HERMIT-SAGE
from: **Unworldly Wind**

Once in a Parking Lot 77
Red Squirrel 78
To Not And Wish You Had 79
Reflections 80
Rose in Window 81
Of What Significance 82
The Chronicler 83
Seeking the Hermit-Sage 84
New England Palms 85

UNWORLDLY WIND
from: **Unworldly Wind**

Winter Cottage 89
Spring Woods 90
After the Spade 91
Strange Harvest 92
Bright Days 93

Herr Stein 94

The Doe 95

Winter Lightning 96

From Now On 97

Another Take on Saturday Morning 98

OF DESTINY AND MOONLIGHT
from: **BLUE NIGHT** *revised*

Of Destiny and Moonlight 101

Past Midnight 102

Enlightenment 103

Night Journey 104

Lacuna 105

At Moonlit Window in Negligee 106

Nude #27 & Musings 107

Meadow Gospel 108

Dropping in On an Old Neighbor 109

New Property 110

The Stonecutter's Daughter 111

Vienna 112

The Photographer & After 113

One Tree Island 114

Loud and Clear 115

At Lew's Sunoco 116

After the Fireworks 117

Downtown Café 118

Woman Playing Guitar 119

Sudden Lyric 120

Waiting and Then Not Waiting for a Green Light
In Greenfield, Massachusetts 121

IV
KEEP ON KEEPING ON
from: **Betrayal On Maple Street**

Keep On Keeping On .... 125 - 130

V
THE TEMPERATURE OF LOVE (a sequence)
from: **Betrayal On Maple Street**

The Temperature of Love 133
The Bruise 134
The Pearl 135
The Compact 136
The Egg & The Pearl 137
An Offering Mean and Poor 138
The Lesson 140
The Loft 141
After the End 142

PEDAL POINT
from: **Unworldly Wind**

Pedal Point .... 145 - 155

PART TWO

from:
ADRIFT
selections from: **BLUE NIGHT**
tanka, cherita, haiku & short free form 159

from:
THIS HUNGER, TISSUE-THIN
tanka 201

from:
OUTER EDGES
cherita 237

from:
IN AN UPSTAIRS ROOM
cherita 261

from:
THE COLORS OF ASH
selected tanka & cherita 293

from:
THE HORIZON WAITS
tanka, cherita, haiku & short free form 323

THUNDER AND APPLE BLOSSOMS
new & selected haiku 363

selected poems 1968 - 2022

PART ONE

TAKING NOTICE

from:
Unworldly Wind

I Step Out on My Porch Near Midnight

Snow,
flecked by moon made mica.

Cold, windless air—even
the roar of the woods
is faint tonight;

And faint, too,
the creak
of my leather jacket—faint

As the rigging of a galleon
heard across the seas of time . . .

While overhead
Orion faintly flickers.

Feeding Chickadees in Winter

Already accustomed to the procedure,
it isn't long till one
flutters down from the sky to clutch
the edge of my hand;

a moment more to twitch and eye
the seed in my palm, select
two or three, and flit away—

        —such delicate talons!

the sensation lingers, engendering
a tenuous ache
        —a millet of love.

Branch after Branch

Slats of clear gold sunlight
and snow like fur on every branch
and every branch after branch after branch
as far as thought can reach . . .

I go to see if our road's been plowed.
The many small birds melt
before my boots and frosty breath.

Branch after branch, vast in its snowy hush,
the universe is as big as you think it is—

and maybe one or two trees more.

Crossing the Connecticut River

A day of rain
in February and
from the bridge
in Sunderland,
the river—

broad and flat
and grey
like gunmetal,
and in parts,
sheening—

the trim of trees
along both banks,
drab plum and
pigment of iron—

very lovely,
very steel,
like a lithograph
in some

old tome—tombed
for posterity.

The Winter Woods

What presences around the cabin pressed
my consciousness through
the ghostly night, that now

in the winter morning sunlight,
like hoary skeletons, tease
the eye? The dead and the dormant

all alike; but come the leafy season,
green by God, will separate the dead
from the living.

Spring Beauties

Each year I mark the stationary progress
made by a cluster of Spring Beauties,
that at a distance are a band
of some religious sect arrayed
in frail lavender gowns, leaning
southward into the nearly impenetrable grass on
an endless pilgrimage, remarkable
for being at once onward yet having
no apparent point of departure or arrival.
I look on, fascinated
by their adherence to a persistent paradox,
and also by what they are—
spring beauties – beautiful flowers.

An Easter Morning

I flung open
the window
one daffodil morning;

in came
the clamoring chimes,
tormenting,

with faulted
intervals,
some weary hymn—

quite suddenly
prodding
a childhood bruise.

Taking Notice after a Long Dark Night

The dew is not yet burned
from the orchard grass—

Crows range the open sky
on easy wings—

To the north,
a chain saw pitch-shifting
gnars a tune—

The forsythia is yellow, the lawn,
salt-crusted with Spring Beauties—

A wasp dangles by—

To the north,
a great conifer falls, sputtering
like firecrackers—

I raise my coffee mug, greet
the acrid bite—

How clear, how crisp the air!

Maple Keys

May caught us in a fall
of maple keys,

showered us with the sting
of pure potential,

rained down her dizzy burden
on our shoulders,

paving this quiet street
with small misfortunes.

Jack-in-the-pulpit

"You kids stop that now.
          You'll harm it sure"—the
Jack-in-the-pulpit by
          Gramma's back porch.

———

O so carefully we scrunched
          the upright Jack,
where he stood like a spike
          in his purple pulpit

'neath that lick of a canopy, only
          to hear his
scritch-scritch-scritch.
          That was his sermon,

you see, and how Jack, the preacher,
          ever survived our
curious fingers, our
          inquisitional thumbs

to evangelize another day,
          is a marvel indeed.

E. H. Shepard's Painting
of Eeyore's Birthday

This framed print reminding me
of childhood playgrounds,
this pastoral scene where
"Pooh and Piglet look on as
Eeyore tries to put the balloon into the jar,"
got stuck in time
and just in time for just
beyond the vanishing point
a threat to childhood brews,
like the foreboding presence of Mordor,
like storm clouds on the horizon
of a picnic.

After Reading an Epic Fantasy

Quite suddenly, full blown,
out of the chubby cheeks of an infant wind,
a leaf landed on a mud-puddle,
like a strange, crude vessel launched
on a fathomless café au lait sea.
It tacked eastward for seven ticks of time
then lost its course in a birthday candle blow.

Later, by the sun-shrunken mud-puddle
that had beached the curled brown leaf,
an ant swam a minuscule cove.
But it was a gigantic monster,
and I saw the horrific peril of yet another episode
in the epic from which I'd been excluded,
too huge to be viewed
even as a comprehensible god.

Paths that Crossed

Along my back porch bannister, teetering
with all the caution of an afternoon bibber,
he carries his barley body with hauteur
above the dust, on eight hair-thin stilts.

In the long, hot afternoon the mind meanders:
   "daddy longlegs (or harvestman if you prefer);
   race: arachnid; color: albino—"

Albino. The mind shouts. The word becomes
the generator and I
the electrical impulse lost
in the terrible circuits
of superstition.   (Will it be plus or minus?)

Nonetheless, with a child-learned deftness
I catch one silver wire and place this aberration,
this frosted transistor
teetering along like a mechanical toy,
on solid ground.

I let him go. I let him go but not
without a shudder and not
without note
in this, our long, dark chronicle, together.

The Weight of One Small Death

When I lifted the dead sparrow
from the lawn, it was light,
incredibly light: lighter
than a sheet of paper; lighter
than the bird alive; nearly lighter
than the weight in hand,
which was light – light
as the thought of a bird.

View from a North Window

For a moment, the sun
on a red barn, dying,
on dry fields still as a gold death-mask
warmed yellow only to the eye
beneath the winter-prophesying sky,
before night's shadow gathers the last straws
of afternoon to its scrawny breast;
the sun on a red barn, dying,
resurrects a lone child, playing.

Each Stone

What they left behind them
are the stone fences.

Each stone,
    now covered by a patina of lichen;
Each stone,
    grayish-green, here,
    in the clean November sunlight;
Each stone,
    once held between two palms.

These stone fences
are their Stonehenge
to us:
miles and miles of hand-felt care
falling back into time
through the clear November air.

November Gold

In the aging afternoon,
at the far edge of the lichen-hued pasture
on which the remnants of last night's
snow lie like tufts of cotton,
the bleak branches of old pear trees brighten,
on and off,
beneath the surfing clouds,
catch November gold
between the surfing clouds,
in the hoary snarl of their broken fingers,
while beyond the pasture and the trees,
fields the color of copper lighten,
on and off,
all as though attached
to some neon advertising apparatus,
quietly flashing the hopeless SOS
of an age,
soon to slip into the western horizon, forever.

from:

A RIVER YEARS
FROM HERE

Haibun and Other Poems

Ballad

There is a river years from here
   That flows without a name,
I sailed my boat between its banks
   For never gold nor fame.

Like Robinson Crusoe all alone,
   Except for a dog named Bruce.
I had no money, no extra clothes,
   No nothing without use.

A jack-knife was my only tool
   A sling-shot was my weapon,
A magnifying glass for fire
   My fate left up to heaven.

I remember well the natives' talk
   By the falls that bear the name
Of whip-poor-wills that disappeared
   Long before I came.

The talk of an enchantment found
   In the woods at the river's source,
An enchantment never proved by me
   Because there came a voice,

A voice as faint as the evening light,
   A voice that called my name,
A compelling voice upon the wind,
   That called until I came,

Came home to supper all muddy from play
   In the creek where I had had
Adventures to tell to the natives I knew,
   Whom I still call Mother and Dad.

There is a River Years from Here

All day, thoughts about a river, years from here,

a creek, really, that flows without a name through the
green-dusk of an ageless woods,

and how I sailed there a galleon,

a halved walnut shell with its wedge of paper sail, beneath
the spread of a great old maple tree, where the
creek pooled below the chicken coops;

and how the leaning woods peered over my shoulder in
those days when salamanders were dragons;

and how I searched for neither gold nor fame,

but for treasures among the water polished pebbles,
despite humidity, mosquitoes, waterstriders,
"dragons,"

and the great granddaddy of a crawfish, who hung out
among the stones, that were really boulders, below
the pool;

and how the chickens just loved a crawfish tossed over

the chicken mesh—but not the great granddaddy,

for it would have been a sin and a shame for such an aged
monster to end up chicken feed.

All day, thoughts about a river, years from here, that flows
without a name.

torrent in Spring
a trickle now—in youth
my Conrad river

The Latch

With its miniature rock gardens, grape arbor, and roses
(roses everywhere, like a child's experiment with rouge);
with its neatly trimmed grass along the flagstone walks;
with its birdbath (strategically placed, as was its willow
tree)—the backyard had all the aura of a formal garden.

In that lawn (just large enough to frame a family portrait),
hemmed in by a wire fence disguised with honeysuckle
vines and marigolds, one somehow achieved a sense of
privacy; even a sense of seclusion from the nearby
neighbors. While outside, a narrow broken alley ran
between two rows of other backyard lawns.

All this (after all these years), like the fragments of a
dream at noontime. Except for the latch. Substantial as a
candy stuck in the throat, the latch remains in mind, as if
I'd just stepped out of that microcosmic Eden into the
narrow alleyway this early morning, closing the gate
behind me with a *click!*; closing the gate behind me *with
all that is before time began* locked! in a single syllable,
for all time.

in a shaded spot
   the ruins
      of a sundial

Steel Town

after devouring fifteen
thousand men daily
the dragon stretches twelve miles
along the river
and sleeps fitfully at night

though its breath poisons our breath
and its belches bruise,
with a plum-rubescent glow,
the black horizon

still we would not murder this
sleeping *brutus* for
its fire bakes our daily bread

Eleven to Seven

night shift—
see that the chute stays open
the mesmerizing spill of ore

the salamander glows cherry red
Camel lit by a touch

night shift—
pulp novel, every second page
dimmed by dust . . .

2 a.m., thermos of coffee
sandwiches, cake

night shift—
3 to 6, the longest hours
2nd pack of cigarettes

over the PA system, an argument
`god-damn hunky'

night shift—
through the sky hole, snowflakes,
the faint gray light of dawn

showered and ready to punch out
"take care, roads are icy . . . "

The Sliver of Steel

When Carl's steam-powered sawmill blew up
in Shade Hollow,
three men were injured, one killed;
and then there was Ed Jacobs,
who walked around as if dazed all afternoon.

And when evening came,
Jack, his brother, found him "out back"
watching a sunset, "unlike himself."

Doc Schaffer found a pink spot
beneath Ed's chin, and a pink spot
on top his head.

The whip-poor-will night found him dead.

Member of the Club

there were 5 of us
   in the hollow
      and every summer there'd be the club

    president
    vice-president
    secretary
    treasurer
    and member

I was always the member

     . . .

one summer
   there were only 4 of us
      so there had to be a

    president
    vice-president
    secretary/treasurer
    and member

      Why?

Consider the Inch-worm

hunch stretch
  bunch reach
    each inch
    a measured movement
    each movement
      a moment's pleasure,
        each sure inch
          by inch—the inch-worm:
          and I, too,
          would find the good
            in each inch of time
              along the branch of always . . . .

Black Ant Experiment

The black ant,
   placed on the chip of Arctic CO_2,
     ran
4 to 5 centimeters
   rapidly slowing
     (a cheap wind-up gadget
quickly spent) till
   frosting over, it stopped;
     froze,
with one leg held high—
   a statuette sculpted of zinc;
     a micro-monument unto itself,
the victim of an idle science.
   And when nudged
     by a childish finger—
broke in half.

The Wasp & The Spider

In the dust a wasp and spider caught
My boyish eye where they grappled and fought

Just when the spider broke free and ran
From the wasp that circled and circled again.

The spider's eight feet bought a foot
More desperate life for him till fate

Turned kamikaze and power dived down
On him. The sting was true! The brown

Back dimpled, doubled, rolled—a stricken
Ball of frenzied splinters, kicking.

The wasp backed away, became poised.
Arch-backed, wings spread, sure of her poison,

Gangly-legged now, her delicate toes
In the dust, she circled the stiffening throes.

The fight was done but I stayed stooped
Until the last leg slowed and stopped.

On the Verge of Autumn

I'd seen her about town often enough—pleasingly plump, neatly dressed, with snow-white hair that belied her age, and such blue eyes. And now we were sharing a store front over-hang against the sudden downpour. She must have been about my age, no more than forty then. A classic merry widow, if widow she was.

To be sure, we talked about the weather and other important things, till at length I found myself saying: *"... but I don't drink wines anymore."* To which she replied, making the moment memorable: *"Oh I know, wine used to make me so romantic, but now I just get spacey."* It was about then that the rain lessened and she decided to chance the drizzle.

As I said, I'd often seen her around the town - often - but after that I never saw her again. The image of her running across the parking lot, in neat spiked-shoes, dodging puddles with a pleasing bounce, a tabloid tented over her snow-white hair, is the last image I have of her.

on a grey day
      in a grey town
            a sprig of asters

And Other Important Things

The meadow rolls away into the woods. The house is hidden below the crest of a straw mulched garden. We are sitting on the sun-warmed grass talking of things soon to be forgotten. Already, I've forgotten the breed names of the penned chickens—the white, the russet, and the dark brown ones with the orange and black plumage behind their necks.

Absent-mindedly, she feeds them grass, one blade at a time, as they mill and chorus a reedy background to our talk. I'll not remember till later how the window of a door onced betrayed her loving gaze on my back.

I tell of my son's first botanical lesson in the woods last week, while the youngest of her two daughters treads barefoot over the glistening straw. When I finish she says: *"There's a small stream down there. It dries up in the summer, but in spring it grows skunk-cabbage and other important things."*

"And other important things," I echo, remembering. And she, too, remembering laughs an old laugh unsettling the present moment momentarily.

As I adapt to the rural mother displacing the urban musician, with whom, shoulder to shoulder, I'd copied manuscripts one winter, the hapless separation I'd held so precious these past five years dissipates without pain or sorrow.

we bid farewell
the white silence
of a falling petal

Evening Walk

The heat still rises from the fields and road mingling the essences of grass and dust. I enjoy these solitary walks after a day of manuscripts and notes.

> *her diary—*
> *if only I hadn't forced*
> *its tiny lock . . .*

The dog runs ahead, circles, explores a field of buckwheat, then checks back with me before another tongue-flapping foray. He always returns as if to explain himself and ask permission.

> *once in a moonlit orchard*
> *what might have been . . .*

A great dead tree stands in arrested motion, as if tossed by an airy turbulence, the perfect sculpture for a stormy life, its barnwood gray set off by forest green.

> *jazz*
> *and the neon, nylon nights—*
> *your fame is everywhere*
> *old friend*
> *I am stretched with longing*

Today, I noticed that autumn's tarnish has touched the tree outside my window. In a month or so, it too, will show its structure.

and the autumn woods
so lovely that you want
but don't know what it is
you want—
it only makes you sorry

The serene violence of the sunset, that flared briefly like an opened forge, is now replaced by a gray veil.

stemless in the dusk
the Queen Anne's lace float—
the path grows luminous

The dog has gone ahead now, not asking for my permission. He will be waiting at the back door. I crest the last hill to home and see an orange moon low in an orchid sky.

as night takes over . . .
walking knee-deep
in the chirring
of crickets

Japanese Lanterns

By the doorstep, so country common a thing to see
—Japanese lanterns. Some five of them, reduced

to their skeletal frame, more delicate than lace,
caging small orange bulbs—bulbs burning bright

by the doorway this dim December afternoon,
suggesting something still to be occasioned.

> snow flurries –
> stacking an arm load
> of firewood

Tidings

Across the room,
the tassel beneath the hanging pot of ivy,

looks like an angel in a hula skirt
come to sing carols from a leafy songbook.

Happy are the objects that make their own poetry
—and happy, too, those who can see

tidings of great joy in a fray of yarn.

   sunlight on red oak
   newspapers heaped
     with ground pine

The Putting Away of Rookie

Pop and Mom

"Pop, you've got to do it soon,
    It isn't right to let
Him suffer. Hear? This afternoon,
    And then you needn't fret."

"You tend your business, Mom, and I'll
    Tend mine," was all he said,
Then poured a coffee, stirred awhile,
    Before he dunked his bread.

Pop and Rookie

"Come here old *Hund*." Pop sat on
    The back porch in the wan
November sun. The dog, upon
    Arthritic legs, had gone

To use the apple tree and now
    He tottered back. "We old'uns
Have got to keep a hold, somehow,
    On all the time we've stolen."

Pop to Kurt

"All right, I guess. I can't complain.
    Mom's been carryin' on
This noon, in regards to Rookie again,
    That's all. I see you've gone

And put the shop in good repair.
 The plumbing craft has passed
Me by with all this new styled hardware.
 That's what I said. Mom sassed

Me good, but she don't see it plain—
 What do you mean, you'll do
It for me? He's in no real pain;
 If there was reason to

I'd tend to it myself. That mean
 Old hound's as good as me."
All this to Kurt who'd never seen
 Pop act but stoically.

About Rookie

Rookie: a khaki-colored hound,
 Born in 'forty-two,
Hence the name; a rover bound
 To be, three times, the view

Some irate farmer held along
 The barrel of a gun;
He shook at sight or sound of one,
 The fear was still so strong.

Mom and Kurt

"Kurt, you've got to do it soon.
 It isn't right to let
Him suffer." "I know. This afternoon,
 Mom, then you needn't fret."

"It's not like Pop to let it go;
    You know he can't abide
A man who puts off duty." "He's slow
    About what he'll decide,

That's all." "There's nothing to decide.
    He knows what must be done."
"He knows but—" "Kurt, he's gone inside
    The shed; you fetch the gun."

Kurt and Rookie
The old dog trembled when he saw
    The sun glint off the rifle,
But struggled to his feet, still trustful
    Of Kurt, whose word was law.

They walked across the copper meadow
    Into the leafless wood;
Among the rags of autumn, below
    The giant oak they stood

A moment, silent, as old friends will,
    Then Kurt began to dig.
When he had finished, the woods was still;
    Kurt pointed with a twig

And Rookie stepped into the ground.
    Above them the white-gold sun
Had tangled in the trees. Kurt found
    It hard to lift the gun.

Pop

As Pop came out into the wan
   November sun he caught
A whiff of wood smoke wafted on
A sharp, west wind, "So autumn's gone
   (He heard the distant shot)
   And winter's come," he thought.

Star

In his ninety-third year he complained of seeing only one star in the sky at night, saying that it was "a sign of the last days," there being only one star in the heavens at night.

"No, Dad," his youngest daughter would say, "It's only your eyes."

But he was not persuaded and would go off to find his dime store glasses, go off to the dining room to read the news by yellow lamplight, while Nora graded papers on the kitchen table, as she had for thirty years. This was in harvest time and the evening star was Venus.

Winter wrapped them warm around the wood fueled range and when the crocuses peeped above the drab grass once more, he again took up his post on the porch at dusk, and with it his same complaint of two seasons past.

"It's your eyes, Dad."

But, "no," it was "a sign," he'd say. And in a way—

What difference to the man who encounters a sign, if the letters are painted on or all but the letters are painted on? The sign still reads the same. Still reads the same.

wild geese overhead –
where the homestead stood
only grass

The Johnstown Flood
May 31, 1889

from:
Unworldly Wind

The Johnstown Flood
May 31, 1889

———

At the beginning only the high waters from the rain swollen rivers
    flooded the streets.

• • •

We had come down to Johnstown the day before to visit with my
    aunt and uncle that lived on Locust Street, and to see the
    Decoration Day celebration, the parade and other
    festivities,

And by then it was late and a long ride home by horse and buggy,

But still we might have gone home that night, but my aunt said:
    "Stay and see the flood," not knowing, because this was
    nothing new to the Johnstown of those days, the high
    rivers and the flooded streets,

And so we stayed the night.

• • •

And the next day we were to go home, but it had been raining hard
    all night,

And the streets were flooded, and the rivers were still rising,

And so we stayed on till noon to see how things would go.

• • •

And after the noon meal, my father and my uncle sat at the kitchen
stove with their boots off and their feet up on a coal
bucket, drying their stocking feet by the heat of the stove.

And I recall their debating whether to free the horses at the nearby
livery stable, as the water had already reached the poor
animals' fetlocks some while ago,

And the waters were still rising,

And the rain continued without ceasing,

But they thought they'd wait and see, not knowing.

• • •

And while they were talking at the kitchen stove, with their feet up
on the coal bucket, the water had begun seeping in under
the door unnoticed, till one of them put his stocking feet
down from the bucket.

• • •

It was then my aunt and mother took my baby brother and me into
the brick building next door,

The brick building that was a millinery, whose upper floors were
the living quarters of the woman who ran the millinery,

Took us to those upper rooms, where I was given a doll to play
with,

And there, in those upper rooms, I sat on a bed playing with the
doll, not knowing,

While my mother, and aunt, and the woman who ran the millinery
talked of this and other floods, not knowing.

• • •

Not knowing, till my mother heard the sound and, through the
upstairs window, saw a wall of water rushing toward us,

A wall of black water rushing toward us, with a long rumbling sound like continuous thunder.

• • •

Knowing now, my mother called down across the yard to warn the men, where they still sat by the stove in the room at the rear of my uncle's house.

And knowing now the truth of her words, my aunt grabbed up my baby brother and took me by the hand,

And not knowing just what, I thought to take the doll with me, but at the last moment put it down on the bed because it wasn't mine,

And knowing not what, the men must have come quickly, for we were all together now,

And quickly we fled the room by an attic stairway,

And just in time, for I remember seeing the front wall burst inward as we clambered up the stairway,

And quickly my father and uncle dragged us with them through an opening to the roof just as the roof lifted and floated away,

Floated away toward the swirling debris in the backed up water at the stone bridge,

Floated for an interminable time, with shouts, and screams, and cries to God, and sorrowful sights all around us.

• • •

And after floating to the stone bridge, not knowing what next,
Clinging to the roof, not knowing what next,
Drifting toward Kernville, not knowing what next,
Our roof broke up and we were forced again to jump and claw our way onto another roof floating nearby,

And after Mother, and Father, and I, not knowing what next, gained that nearby roof (though we nearly lost Mother to the black water),

And after leaving behind my aunt, my uncle, my baby brother, clinging to the broken roof,

And after floating in interminable fear on the endless debris-strewn water, amid the cries and supplications, not knowing what next,

And after seeing the three left behind rescued at an upper window of a school building on Napoleon Street,

I looked up into my father's troubled face (I can still see that face today) and though I was only five years old, I said, knowing it was so, *"Papa, God will save us,"* and he answered, *"Yes."*

. . .

But we were not safe yet, there was a time still to drift with what sights and sounds around us I cannot say, though

I can still see a woman in a flaming church steeple
I can still see her waving arms—
I can still see no one to rescue her—
I can still see her leap into the water—
I cannot erase from my mind this woman, trapped by water in the flaming church steeple.

. . .

And there was debris of every sort,
And there were shrieks and crying outs of every sort,
And there were others on roofs, like ourselves, and
There was nothing you could do,
There was nothing you could do for others,
There was nothing you could do but pray.

. . .

And then there was a house across the street from the school building where my aunt, my uncle, and my baby brother had been rescued,

And there we floated, finally,

And there we were also helped through a window to a second-story room,

And there, a woman in that house gave dry clothing to my mother and put her to bed, for my mother had been badly lacerated when my father had pulled her onto the second roof, and she was surely in shock,

And there I remembered the doll I'd left behind because I'd been taught not to take what wasn't mine (it spites me to this day).

• • •

And then I had an intense desire for a drink of water, and begged and begged, till the woman in that house gave me water from the tap,

But it was muddy and did not stay down.

• • •

And then I was persuaded to lie across the bed at my mother's feet,

And there I lay hearing the groans and cries and the crushing of buildings that went down in the water outside,

And saw that the sky was lurid (but did not know that it was from the burning wreckage at the stone bridge till later)

And then I slept till morning.

• • •

Of the day after I can remember waist deep water, and men making walkways of boards,

And people going over the walkways to the hills,

And our family helped to Sherman Street, where another uncle gave us food and loaned us a horse and buggy,

And I can remember the four hour trip home at night, and the moonlight and the large, fleecy clouds,

And can still see the cloud shadows coming and going on the hillsides, and remember my fear of the shadows moving toward me,

My fear that they would engulf me as the flood had engulfed so many the day before,

But I never let on.

. . .

And when we were almost home we met another uncle on his way to Johnstown with a wagon load of supplies,

How they knew to do so, how they'd heard of the flood, I don't know,

There weren't any telephones in those days,

Not way out in the country where we were:

. . .

Yes, of the day after, I can remember all that, that

And my greatest loss—the doll.

Rosa Pearl Zimmerman Bowman (1884 - 1975) was the author's maternal grandmother. This prose poem is based on a taped account, as well as the author's memory of many tellings.

THE WINTER OWL

THE WINTER OWL

The windowpanes were edged in frost, and we
Four cousins bunched to see the screech owl perched
On an apple branch above the drifted snow.

"He might be sick," Kate said.
                              "No! He's sleeping.
He's just sleeping," Freddy replied.
                                    "He's most
Likely hungry," Gramma put in. "Poor thing,
They don't often come in this close to dwellings
Unless they can't find food in winter."
                                        "Do you
Think he's starving?" Kate frowned.
                                    "I'll put some hamburg
Out in a moment," Gramma answered.
                                   "Won't
He freeze?" Bess wondered.
                          "Yeah. How do we know
He isn't frozen dead already?" I asked.

"He was alive this morning," Gramma said.
"I thought for sure he'd frighten off when Pop
 Shoveled the path, but all he did was close
 His eyes and turn his head as if he scorned

To watch." Then Gramma, crossing to the yellow
Stove that drew its heat from naphtha, added,
"You kids go play in the dining room. I can't
Have you bouncing around in here, you'll make
The dough fall."
                        Wet cloths covered pans of rising
Dough on the kitchen's two broad radiators.
"He'll freeze," decided Bess.

                        "He'll be all right,"
Said Freddy, "as soon as he gets something to eat."

                · · ·

In the dining room, around the walnut table,
In the circle of the chandelier's dim light,
We kids became jewel merchants.

                                        A wealth
Of buttons spilled from a quart tin box, and we
Were in business. Fev'rishly we sorted through them;
Scrutinizing each with an expert's eye;
Watchful for a button's value in
Another's eye; haggling, threat'ning, shouting—
"I saw it first!"
                        "No you didn't!"

                                        —till from
The kitchen this ultimatum:

                                        "If you kids
Can't get along in there, you can put the buttons
Back in the box this minute."
                                        We got along.
We valued the buttons at more than bickering,
Being allowed to keep one button each,
Each time the buttons were allowed.

                                            I found
The best button ever, that day, a gilt
Edged hexagon (most likely brass), framing
A thumbnail opal Abstract, with an eyelet
Behind and so not marred by sewing holes.
A great find destined to button, some other day,
The simple fabric of a priceless lesson.

                    . . .

At noon, we found the kitchen table changed.
The pans and mixing bowls, the sifted flour,
The rolling pin, the measuring cups—all gone.
And in their place were jars of jam, a patty
Of home churned butter, and Betsy's own rich milk
In a pitcher, and cold stewed apples, and warm bread
So fresh you could roll it back to dough between
Your thumb and index finger, and for dessert—
The promise of one cinnamon roll apiece.

"He's so small. Do you think he's a baby owl?"
Kate asked—I answered, "He's a screech owl. That's as
Big as they get."
                    "Still he's awfully small."

We all peered out the frosted window and saw
The winter owl still perched on the low branch
Above the pathway cut through knee-deep snow.

"Did he eat any of the hamburg?"
                                    "Not that
I noticed, Kate."

"I hope he isn't sick."

"Why would he be sick?" Freddy wanted
To know. But no one knew or no one said.
Then Gramma ladled out the barley soup,
A steaming bowl for each of us.
                              "Now don't go
Bolting your food, Michael," she said to me.
"You don't get all the nourishment you should,
Eating so fast."
                    I slowed down as best
I could.
          "Wasn't he scared of you, when you
Put out the meat?" Kate asked.
                              "I was afraid
He'd flush, but he never so much as blinked an eye."

"That's because he's sleeping," Freddy insisted.

"Couldn't we bring him in?" Kate asked.
                              "Let's give him
A chance to feed on his own and then we'll see.
And stay away from the window," Gramma added.
"He can probably see our movements in the house."

I couldn't help but feel the wintry scene
Beyond the frosted window. I liked the look
Of the tangled apple branches etched against
The gray-white sky, and the hillside's snowy sweep
With only charcoal-sketch suggestions of what
The world had been before the age of snow.
But it was the owl who made the afternoon.

On the twigged branch that sloped over the path,
Like an arm reaching down to lend a hand,
He slept—hunched with cold. And as I watched him,
A feeling, dark and deep, stole over me,
The kind you get from a grim tale told at bedtime,
The kind I got from the dark painting hung
In Gramma's living room.
                              "He might be too weak
To feed himself," Bess posed. But no one answered.
We were busy with soup and arguments
Of what to do that afternoon, while Gramma
Sipped her coffee lost in thought. And then,
As promised, one cinnamon roll for each of us.

                    . . .

The stairway opened both onto the kitchen
And the living room, and with the door shut to
The kitchen but open to the living room,
We played a button game which we called "school."

Kate was the teacher first, and stood facing
Her pupils—Freddy, Bess, and me—who sat
Crowded together on the first of the two
Steps to the landing. Behind her back she changed
A button from hand to hand a number of times,
Then held her hands straight out in front of her
For me to guess which hand it was that held
The button.
                  Each step was like a grade in school,
And you progressed from grade to grade by right
Guesses. A wrong guess kept you where you were,
And two wrong guesses put you back a grade,

Unless, of course, you were already on
The bottom step. I made my guess. Kate flashed
An empty hand—"Too bad"— then mixed the button
Behind her back a second time to test
The next student—Freddy. And so it went.

I enjoyed this game as much as any, but
That afternoon with the dim of winter at
The windows and the living room in dusk,
As it always was, but even more so that day,
I couldn't keep my attention on the game.
Above the old upright piano hung
The painting that had always haunted me.
Inside its gilt frame all was night, and shadow
Within shadow, and a yellow moon
Fleecing the night clouds above a black castle,
A castle so deep in shadow that I knew
Of its existence only because I'd climbed
On top the piano once to see up close
What the picture was about. It had been painted
Years ago by a relative long deceased.
And looking at the painting that afternoon,
I wondered who she was and felt a dark
Something, the same as I had felt at lunch time,
Looking out the frosted window at
The sleeping screech owl on the apple branch.
It was a brooding mood that made me want
To be alone.
                            So after a few more turns
I quit. I said I didn't feel like playing
Anymore, and that made Freddy mad
At me. But Kate said that a person had

A right to their own feelings no matter what
Those feelings were. And I agreed with her.

                    . . .

In the kitchen, looking out the frosted window
To see the owl, I saw how dim, how dark
The afternoon had grown, and guessed more snow
Was on its way, and next I saw the owl
Still perched among the wickerwork of twigs,
And though a gust of wind ruffed his feathers,
He still sat on, supremely unperturbed.

"I wouldn't hang around the window, Michael,"
Said Gramma. "Our movements in the house might make
Him fearful."
                    I stepped back, but waited for
That sense of brooding to come over me
Cloud-shadow-like, and when it did, I left
The kitchen window for the living room.
The game was over. But Freddy still wouldnt talk
To me. Then Bess said that she was "tahred" and laid
Down on the braided rug between the living
And dining rooms.
                    "You'll catch a cold," Kate told her.
"I don't care."
                    "Get up, Bess, or I'll tell Mother
When we get home."
                    So Bess got up, and for
A time we milled around the dining room,
Argumentative and bored, till finally
We gathered at the frosted kitchen window.

"Did he eat the hamburg?" Freddy asked of Gramma.

"He hasn't touched it, so far as I can tell."

"Do you think he's sick or just hungry?" Bess
Wanted to know.
                  "If he was just hungry,"
Kate said, "I think by now, he would have tried
To eat the hamburg."
                       "Unless he's afraid of us,"
I said. "He probably can see our movements
In the house."
                We all stepped back a step into
The dimness of the kitchen. Then Gramma said,
"I'll just go out and bring the poor thing in.
I can't see sense in waiting any longer.
Bess might be right, that he's too weak to feed
Himself."
              We gathered close around the window
To watch. First, a bitter cold burst in on
The kitchen's fragrant moisty-warmth, and next,
We saw Gramma cross the porch and step down
Into the pathway cut through knee-deep snow.
We watched, and the wind flapped Gramma's apron, and
A few grey hairs streamed from her bun. We watched,
And the owl sat stock-still with his eyes closed tight,
Right over that narrow path where Gramma walked.
I watched. My guts electric waiting for
The burst of feathers that would happen at
The moment of capture.
                   But when Gramma reached
Up for the sleeping owl there was no burst

Of feathers, no effort at flight, or attempt to flee,
No struggle of any kind.
                              Gramma had simply
Reached up and taken down the owl from his perch,
The way you'd take a jar down from a cupboard
Shelf. And when she reentered the kitchen's warmth,
Holding the little owl so close, she said,
"I blame myself. I should have acted sooner."

A CUP FULL OF SEASONS

from:
Unworldly Wind

A Cup Full of Seasons

The cup
was a tin cup bearing
in bas-relief a cast
of five figures from
a nursery rhyme.

First Season
At breakfast on cold mornings
sitting by the oven
getting warm enough on one side
for both sides
and looking out the frosted window
over snow-laden hills
to hills ice-blue in the distance
and being cozy beside the oven
scorched on one side
still shivering on the left
I'd drink my dark brown Postum
hot from that Winter cup.

Second Season
Over the fresh plowed field
by the fence line
where trees grew

with barbed wire deep in their guts
and brush grew up through stones
picked and piled there
from years of spring-plowed fields
ending along the fence line
where the dying cherry tree loomed over
the budding dogwood
where the maple sap ran down
the elderberry spouts
to drip into buckets
that sat on stacks of stone
there I'd take a taste of sugar water
cold and sweet from that Spring tin cup.

Third Season

Down by the barn in summer
towards evening
big green flies caroused the manure pile
outside the small barn
that held some rats, an uncle's car
and standing big-eyed and docile
in the dusky stall the cow named Betsy
who allowed herself to be milked by Grammy
who sitting on a three-legged stool
in the dusky stall milked Betsy
amongst the fragrant hay and dung
the first squirts torrent sounding
in the hollow bucket
there amongst the dust of chaff and straw
I'd have a Summer cup
of animal warm and frothy milk.

Fourth Season
Up hollow
below the Mennonite Church
down the road a way by the creek
where we had fished
for chubs and minnows the summer long
in the shade of the giant oak
its red leaves falling now
down on the weathered building
blowing inside the weathered building
right there in autumn
with all the good smell of apples
ripe and bouncing up the clanking belt
spilling red from the clanking belt
tumbling down to the grinding
clattering machinery below
right there in autumn
I'd have an Autumn cup of cider
sweet and warm from that noisy press.

    The cup
    was a tin cup bearing
    in bas-relief a cast
    of five figures from
    a nursery rhyme.

Posterity

I once found a butterfly whose wingspan was a good three
inches of untold   colors—a butterfly like the paper
airplanes I used to decorate, then toss from the porch
to fly

        high over the dirt road below,

        and

        high over the field beyond;

                the field cropped by Betsy the cow;

                the field with spindly thistles

                        like scaled-down radio towers—

like those airplanes whose wings,

        wings crayon-ornamented or tablet-ruled;

        wings that cut the air, that razor-slit a slot to slip
through, beneath that strange sunlight peculiar to August
Sunday afternoons—

like those airplanes,

        —the butterfly, whose wings in death were fixed
for flight.

Catnip Tea

When your mother sent for Granma,
it was *ring around the rosy* as rosy you lay
in bed between the twisted sheets, for
the sure notion of that grave gentleman

was yours. But after Granma came
and frisked you for flushes and fevers
and gave her prescription (which was a kind
of diagnosis and prognosis, as well),

gave her prescription in those two
familiar words—CATNIP TEA—you
ascertained you'd not be needing
a winding sheet; gleaned you'd be oki-dokie

real soon; fathomed you'd resurrect next day—
and you did.

Home Of The Brave

For three days Grandma's best milker frothed
at the mouth, then died—clearly poisoned. A year
later, old Mike Kovitch, with a skin full, said:
"It a shame about that cow, someday I tell you

Mister Mahler," and so we knew what we already
knew, and Grandpa spoke true when he told us
a desire to see justice done would only result in
something else dying or burning down, and all

Grandma had said to old Mama Kovitch was:
"Those aren't your cherries to pick," it being
Grandma's one cherry tree and she counting on
the crop for preserves, and old Mama Kovitch

had gone off mumbling: *"Me think this free
country,"* no different than any other time.

In Memoriam
John Ira Bowman 1884-1974

Aged ninety, he said to Milly, his daughter,
"Something goes out of life when a man can't
plan his work the night before and see it
through tomorrow." Later that year, shortly

after the untimely passing of a son-in-law,
he said, *"Milly, now there'll be someone*
over there to meet me." And that night
the last of the strokes took him, taking

a week to do so. I believe life to be
a continuum, and having experience
of others gone before me, why not him?
Sometimes I think a stern grandfather

(still the very image of a stoic) frowns down
on once-honed tools that I've let rust.

Wooden Chain

Found in an attic and given to me, years back,
this wooden chain of three links, holding
the shackle of a lantern-like cage, a cage
of four corner-bars that hold, in turn,

a wooden ball the size of a marble, on which you
can see the fly-eye faceted flatness of
the knife's work, yet perfectly round, and all
this marvel carved from a single piece of wood.

I ponder its pedigree, as no one remembers
who carved it, and ponder, too, how the works
of an artist live on, have a life of their own,
taking their chances about the same as any

progeny, and further ask why it is
that old half-known things so tease the mind?

———

clasping my dad's hand
as once he gripped his father's hand
whose hand had once . . .

The Class Ring

I hold in my hand a ring. Moxium High.
Class of '58. The initials my own.
Within weeks, I'd left it by a public sink.
Loss noted and steps retraced—both

immediate, but ... *c'est la vie*. Seven
years later it returned, having found
its way to the alma mater with its
postal pedigree, some half-dozen

other Moxiums. A worthy scholarship,
the particulars of that seven year odyssey,
which remains mute within the zero of
this prodigal trinket of youth, inanimate

wanderer, whose encircled secret rests
upon my palm, yet forever beyond my grasp.

October Elegy

After the burial she walked with me,
Where tall trees, standing in a clear
Sunlight, cast strict shadows across
The drive—a woman just past fifty,
Elegant and gracious, lovely to see.

"You came all the way from Maine, they say.
You must have been very fond of Kurt,"
Meaning her brother, my uncle by marriage,
                        and that was true.

A far hill seemed the reds and golds
Of an old tapestry kicked against
The horizon, while the branches near
At hand were clad in tatters, and one
Old oak in rags of penny-brown.

"You were just a boy when I left home."

That, too, was true, and true still,
The infatuation a boy once felt
For her—though now as mellow as
A bronze medallion smoothed by the wear
                        of a quarter century.

She took my arm, her white-gloved hand
Around my sleeve, and we walked awhile
In silence. Her step was steady, stately,

Despite the cant of her narrow heels
On the cinder drive. And leaving the drive
We crossed a quilt of yellow leaves,
Dimly reflected in the branches
Overhead, and I was made
Momentarily giddy by
                    the lightness of its color.

And as we joined the others, she let
Go of my arm, saying, "I must
See Joan before I leave," meaning
My aunt, her sister-in-law, and smiling
A smile of October charm she left me.

All that was eighteen years ago,
And now I am her age then, and now
I do not think that I shall ever
See her again, and that, I allow,
Is as it should be, now as the reds
And golds of old tapestry
Return, once more, to distant hills—
                    the same but not the same.

Regret

Rosa Pearl Zimmerman Bowman 1884-1975

The log house, also, the homestead,
seemed smaller with the furniture gone.
And in the empty room that was once the kitchen,
there was a scrape mark, a crescent scar, worn
in the wide-plank floor
           "... and all I can figure is,
Grammy must've, for years, dragged
her foot getting up from the table. She had
such bad arthritis, you recall,
and she could never sit still for a moment,
always doing for others ... "
           And I did
recall, that and other things—

And if I could see her again ... if I
could see her again, I would not be impatient;
if I could see her.

Seeking the Hermit-Sage

from:
Unworldly Wind

Once In A Parking Lot

"... my stress lay on the incidents in the development
of a soul: little else is worth study ..." ROBERT BROWNING

Talking in the parking lot across
from the library, where it is shaded
by tall maples, we hear this *chit-chit-chit*
and, wondering, we look up and see a squirrel

watching us from a high branch,
while rotating the nut he's gnawing at.
Seeing us see him, he stops his eating,
stops his busy little teeth, and stops

the *chit-chit-chit*. Silence. Eyes meet eyes.
Then ... he scampers to a higher branch—
and we? I don't remember what we said
or did that day, after the squirrel, or before

the squirrel. Recall only an incident
whose soul-value was its greater value.

Red Squirrel

In summer sunlight the red squirrel scoots up
and down the apple tree, free from all concern,
while the cat watches from the window, and
I from behind the screendoor. Next he runs

along his highway through the greeny treetops,
his highway in the sky, his highway
invisible to me, once run. And now he
takes the shortcut home, leaving branches jostling,

where he's leapt from tree to leafy tree—not
suspecting all the eyes that tracked him. I
suspect we, too, live free of inhibitions
we might otherwise be feeling, if we but knew . . .

And now on ground he swirls
                    around around
            and rounds the corner,
            like water
                        down
                        a
                        drain

                        .

To Not And Wish You Had

Think of it. Jenny Wade. The only
civilian causality of that three day battle
at Gettysburg, eighteen-sixty-three.
Killed in a kitchen while baking bread.

Killed by a bullet that strayed through the door,
which, as a lad, I saw, and the hole, too,
that the bullet made, enlarged and worn smooth
by all the fingers that had verified

the fact. I did not, myself, with finger, further
wear away the truth, for propriety's
own sake. (For we, I understood, were not
so common as to do as common does.)

But I wish I had. Still, to not and wish
you had, is also an experience.

––––––

      thirty long winters
      a misplaced fidelity
      still rankles

Reflections

In the dark depth of the one clear
pane of nine, I saw her love gaze
on the back of me, and in that same clear
glass, looked her in the face—saw

her darkly, until she saw that I
watched her and turned those loving
eyes aside. And when I turned to
face her, in the here and now, I saw

nothing of this affection. O,
her loveliness was ever hers,
and her cheer was ever mine, but
we were never again so intimate

as when we met in that clear, black glass—
that dark,
                    ethereal
                              otherworld.

———

       frost-starred window -
       I stare through my reflection
       into the moonlit orchard

Rose In Window

A small snow sprinkles down—dandruff
through scraggly trees—and dawn's gray
effusion grieves for lack of color,
lack of warmth, lack of leaves, for lack

of all, but also framed within
the window, a narrow stem, sprouting
up from an oboe vase to end
in a ruby explosion or

a scarlet napkin, unfolding.
Against the lack you are too
richly crimson, rose in the window.
You are a red, red torch in the midst

of a dim awakening—yes, rose you are
and are beyond all reason.

Of What Significance

For some years now, this phantom tableau, often seen.
A knight; a snowy field; a barberry bush,
its red berries bright above the snow, but
prickly to the eye without its leaves. The knight

on a palfrey beside the bush, and all environed
by clear air and hush of snow—an expanse
of snow bounded by a distant smudge. A smudge
which is forest. And like the forest, the middle-

distance vague, as well. Details adverting
from any tic to know, like peripheral
presences which will not be confronted with
a stare. Turn, and like that! they aren't. Unlike

the knight; the snowy field; the barberry bush;
and this—words without voice—this: "The Christ Child."

The Chronicler

Quill, scriptorium, ink of pokeberry,
a lasting stack of parchment. I see myself
in a tower overlooking a mountain pass,
with a ribbon of road below that follows

the twisting glint of a khaki river. A scant
traffic passes—carts, wagons, families on foot—
from which I deduce fires, famine, armies
out of control. A world in flux

or ended. Another not perceptibly begun—
begun, regardless, in this scripting now
of a past for what future? Have I brothers?
No matter. A lavender twilight enthralls me,

enchants this hour of my lonely work. I
am he who lives to scribe the chronicle.

Seeking The Hermit-Sage

I see myself on a mountain, an old man
loafing in sunlight, who long since came seeking
the hermit-sage, who not finding him,
lingered, among the pines, a night, a day,

another night and day, to this very hour.
Loafing, I finger the beads of incidents past:
recall the earth-cave found beneath an oak;
the foraged-food enough; and the learned-fire,

friend against winter; the rude hut built;
and the quieting of mind, which I compare
to the slow clearing of muddied water. And now,
on this ledge, as an old man reflecting, loafing

in sun-warmth, it simply comes to me that I
am he, found at last—the hermit-sage.

New England Palms

Somewhere between weed and tree, the sumacs that jungle my
unkempt property. I like them. My neighbors don't. I call them
New England palms.

cliffside cottage
blue hills in the distance
here I could be
a Ryōkan
or a Han Shan

Unworldly Wind

from:
Unworldly Wind

Winter Cottage

Unworldly wind, and dark the midnight forest. So cold the branches click like antlers. Beyond that, not much to know.

in the black of nothing –
        phantom bucks
                battle

Spring Woods

Skunk-cabbages that yesterday were green napkins folded
to stand upright, now forge the bog, swarm the wooded
hillside . . .

> across the path
> a snake
> too cold to care

After the Spade

Tossed and meant for the field, but hanging looped and limp from an apple bough, the snake's carcass.

after the spade
three inches and the tongue
still flickering

Strange Harvest

His first day home on the farm, unscathed by combat, he
loses an arm to the combine harvester.

last night
a sister's auburn hair
this morning white

Bright Days

Bright days, hand-in-hand—what a friendship we had then! You said, "The river is shampooing its hair," and we played Pooh sticks from its bridge.

      that glint

         in the forest –

            where did it go?

Herr Stein

I can still hear Herr Stein saying: " ... but it is a good F, in fact, if there was such a thing as an F+, that's what it would be."

> at the nursing home
> explaining myself
> to a puzzled man . . .

The Doe

As the headlights touch her, her legs fold to unfold on the far side of the fence where she isn't . . . having vanished into thin dusk . . .

gone -
but the wonder
of blood and spirit
remains

Winter Lightning

_____

Revealed as being himself, I hate a favorite uncle for not
quite being my childhood hero.

talking of old times
as dusk crowds the kitchen window
winter lightning

_____

From Now On

_____

She sleeps beside me bathed in moonlight. Saw what I
saw, know what I know. Great sex still, but no heart
for lovemaking.

is this it?
an empty canoe
on a river
slow
as from now on

_____

Another Take on Saturday Morning

Would like to be dark-haired, handsome, lean as a hickory, famous, and have a sense of well being—all on the same day.

greying at the temple
and still "the poem"
unwritten

Of Destiny and Moonlight

from:
Blue Night

Of Destiny and Moonlight

In the moonlight the quilt has no color.
Is a patchwork of different darks, only.

In the woods the hoot owls are calling each
to each and my destiny is three score spent.

This afternoon you visited, wanting to talk
of old times. It seemed an adultery to comply.

Lying here, awake in the moonlight,
I recall an ingot of sunlight that lay

on the floor between us, a wrenched geometry
of gold that could not be lifted.

Past Midnight

Past midnight, I turn off the lamp,
sit listening to the wind. Christmas tree lights

make fern shadows of spruce branches
on the ceiling. Somewhere,

in the vastness of night, the young poet
who will become my friend,

the famous actress I will never meet.

Enlightenment

A disc the yellow of old ivory, and then,
for the first time in a life oblivious,

it comes into focus, the face of the man
in the moon. Not just a disease of pock

and shadow, but the full faced caricature,
the same as seen by you, unknown illustrator

of my Mother Goose, fellow artist
once maligned – now vindicated.

Night Journey

Unable to sleep
I stand at the northeast window.   A pond
of snow-melt,
      backdropped by five spruces
      with a streetlight just beyond,
swamps the lawn—is a lake
where moonlight,
      shredded by the ragged top
      of a midnight forest,
paves,
      with golden cobble stone,
a pathway from glacial shores into the dark
of myth and mystery,
         into the very Land of Færy.

Lacuna

And in those days,
when living as if there were no tomorrow,

I woke not to a new day, but rather to the rewinding
of a watch. On the wall of the room where I slept

and changed clothes hung a three week calendar
that skipped to someday.   Podunk and Now.

At Moonlit Window in Negligee

Secretly, through slitted eyes, I watch.
Once in the Strasbourg cathedral she drew me

into a niche and put my hand where she needed me.
Since then all that was romantic in me has

fallen away. Cliff into ocean. Put your ear
to the conch shell of my used to be.

Nude #27 & Musings

She has turned from a dormer window, clothed
in a sheen of sweat, peach in hand. This world

of dust, indeed. If fruit grew on mountain cliffs,
I'd turn recluse. You know I would. But here

in the fertile, I wipe my chin, endure her mocking eyes.
Fear some unspittable aftertaste.

Meadow Gospel

Where the grass is luxurious, she lies
with an arm across her eyes, her skirt to mid-thigh.

What the mind can't spit, you live with
as a kind of shrapnel or you digest it. Food

for a healing growth. Enabled by the cooperation
of opposing wings, a butterfly lilts about her.

Dropping in On an Old Neighbor

Once promiscuous as a carnival ride she spends
her days in a trailer watching television and smoking

five packs of cigarettes. Thin as a rail and hollow eyed,
she doesn't remember me, and I wonder that I ever thought

her erotic. From her tin can hovel, canned laughter
follows me down the moon bright path.

New Property

Scent of hot grasses. The sun a coin
of molten electrum. In a white dress

of thin muslin, her areolae bloom
dark as the plums warm from the tree.

With a thirst like this there's no help for it.
You thieve and wipe your chin,
laughing at the myth of ownership.

      . . .

    Wicked pretty
    with eyes the blue
    of burning alcohol,
    eyes
    to fuck a heart.

The Stonecutter's Daughter

Well, he was a great artist,
so he could
(when he passed that beaten farm house)
think – *"God, that little girl's in there."*

and all day think,
'how that young girl was there'

that young girl captured in time
captured in aching temperas,
                          for all time.
             . . .

    "working up on the farm
    we go topless

    my uncle doesn't mind"

    umpteen ages since
    still playing
    this over in my mind

Vienna

that room –
can't remember
if there were pictures on the wall

can remember
how it was to enter her

the deliciousness
*

nude
in a stifling room
she opens her legs

positions the cello

outside, the sticky sound
of mid-day traffic
*

arriving by shaded streets

the apartment empty
no forwarding address

how it ended
one Viennese
afternoon

The Photographer & **After**

outside the concert hall, after *The Photographer*,
Glass shattered by a taxi's blare.

at the reception,
   a tinkle of ice in cocktail glasses, as across
    the room a woman lifts her wine glass
      at the very moment I lift mine—world wide,
        how many others? and what might Philip
         be doing this very moment—wherever?

later,
in the square, a frozen fountain spirts,
making of itself an ice palace.

once,
walking winter streets past
yellow window shades, the perfect female profile
          - happened!

once,
outside a Fasching party on Gaisberg—stars
the size of Christmas lights.

  think of it!
to have been Mohr & Gruber, to have written
       Silent Night

One Tree Island

holding my eye
she undoes her blouse
my strict attention

an arch smile
then photons clothe her

wavelets lapping toes
the forest lake
there to receive her

wading out
till her breasts float
voices

diving under
a flash of bare bottom

she waves
from the one tree island
an exaltation of larks

———

in a shade of pines along the lake's edge
I clothe her
in a bikini of kisses

Loud and Clear,

from the dressing booth
at the Railroad Salvage warehouse,
                    this exchange—

"It's cold in here."
"I know it. And I don't got
no bra on neither."

                    —giving shape
to a pointless morning.

At Lew's Sunoco

"Fill it up and check the battery."
  "Fill 'er up?"
   "And check the battery."
    "Right. Fill 'er up."

Across the street
  lawn louts lounge on the grass
   before St. Anne's.

A pigeon detaches itself
  from the sunlit campanile
   circles
    (a fleck of grey weather)
     and returns
      to the yellow brick ledge.

Pop's raw clumped hand,
  a root accepting
   the foliage of commerce—

and the battery goes unchecked.

After the Fireworks,

in blind night, draining
from field to parking lot,
the 4th of July crowd murmurs
over a system of sidewalks;

its camaraderie expressed
in one syllable fixed
(on successive lips) at the lip
of a curb and "curb" that syllable,
like a ripple on a stream,
or a culture—generation unto
generation

Downtown Café

Two raindrops
rivulet down
the café window—

Two tears meet,
one drinks the other,
takes a moment
to digest,
then runs away
with the sum.

Woman Playing Guitar

Her breast
fit
like a fruit

in the curve
of the small guitar,

and I
would have been
her Picasso,

some
Spanish afternoon.

Sudden Lyric

I wake to a daffodil morning
and to the first day of my seventeenth year.
Overnight,
spiders have pitched camp across the lawn
– hoary napkins of silk and dew.

Today we will sing (lugubriously),
   "Up from the grave He rose,
   With a mighty triumph o'er His foes"
and I will love it.

      . . .

Thirty years hence,
I will recall this unforgettable morning,

where a bite-sized Casablanca fan pinwheels,
awry and wee,
   in the lustre of a coffee spoon—

where my wife, not yet born, leans back
from strawberries and cream, laughing
      at my licentious wit—

where two wires cross and part
in some unknowable circuitry.

Waiting and Then Not Waiting for a Green Light
In Greenfield, Massachusetts

The red pulse of three turn signals and the click of my own
      —a serial music, more for the eye than the ear.

Images of unseen birds sweep the rear window of the car ahead,
like a school of neon tetras through an aquarium glass,
but swif' swift—each concise image pulled awry,
as the flock, itself, is warped, is bulged—is gone.

An hour ago: Gray whispery wisp of a man standing
a little less than the librarian on duty:
     " ... I have always been very sensitive,
very creative —yes-yes— have been all my life,
very sensitive, very creative ... " and on the street
outside the library, a drunk grabbed a parking meter,
stiffened—heaved

                           —well there you have it,
a hot lunch.   And now it is—the awaited shift from red
to green—the tachometer needle jumps.
                           (When you redline
on fear you redline, and everybody has a battlefield,
and it doesn't matter where or what the battlefield
when you redline).
                 I still have 20 minutes on a meter
in Brattleboro—but that's another town, another state.

"REDLINE MY HEART 3-PERSONED GOD!" I'm coming home,
home to meat and potatoes and look at that!—
        old apple tree? or bonsai and me incredibly shrunk?

All these years, I have been wasting, wasting, wasting the poem.

KEEP ON KEEPING ON

from:
Betrayal On Maple Street

Keep On Keeping On

Making my way along the winter streets
at the violet edge of day, enticed
by neon, flickering deceits
that keep me keeping one foot further on;
I don't recall—never knew the reasons,
scarcely see the change of season
anymore—

                  more and more,
this monotony of hours
spent in rundown downtown bars
erodes like water from a dripping tap.

In an alleyway,
between a church and all night bakery, I stop
to light a cigarette—

                  And there, stirred
by a *Föhn* of oven fragrance, I recall,
I once had what I wanted,
but still wanted and wanted what?
I never knew.

              And there, for a moment, stirred
by an air of fresh baked bread, I embrace a time
by time distorted—a mere *Gasthaus* of a town
so briefly dwelt in, this pinprick *Heimweh*
is not mine to say.

              Then wondering

if there might not be some brand new brand of aspirin
to stump this seven year long ache
for an amputated youth, I step, again,
into the evening wind, wanting again,
and again not knowing what I want, feeling
inside my chest, again,
the smoke's familiar tightness, again knowing
the city's limits—
that nowhere to go, no one to know feeling.

* * *

At last, or finally, I sit once more,
couched in the rumble of a tavern,
booths along one wall,
a bar, bar stools and all
the people together
doing the same thing together
not needing to speak together
to be together.
Strangers in companionship
—that's a tavern, and shaded lights
and perchance sights
of certain wiles and certain smiles, and guiles
all hip and lipstick;
the body warmth; the smell of beer and smoke;
the signs
concerning ales and wines,
the electric signs
of whiskeys, tonics, gins, and Coke;
and perchance the chance
to slip into companionship.
But even this glow passes,

and you're left among the glasses
that froth and ring the table tops.

Her drink is tasted; mine is gone,
another ordered; the cluttered mirror betrays
a calculating gaze;
then with familiar disgust I follow
the forlorn ploys that ply me onward,
onward to the roads I've traveled
to turn the turns ahead.

I always hoped beyond the bend—
I know it is the same beyond the bend,
always and all the same,
but still I wait to go around again,
though the meaning's grown lame,
of late.

However, it's not roads or women I speak about,
couched here amid this cloud of mumble-jumble, rent,
from time to time, by shrieks of lightning laughter;
couched here among the ocher glasses
that having frothed go flat; here
where the jukebox blurts its not uncommon malady. No,
roads and women are not my meaning, but
seeing as the skit's begun,
I speak the famous line, and so receive
the fateful answer that taunts me more to cling
a moment longer for a further fling.

Although, what difference?—
this long straight stretch of track I'm on just steady narrows into distance.

* * *

While we walk the empty streets
I want to talk;—again, I want to speak;
I want to share with her or someone anywhere
some small conceit
such as has cut me through, complete,
the way a glint off metal cuts the eye by day;
I want to say:

"Yesterday, soft as smoke in the gunmetal sky,
one pink wisp flit and died
as tall and taller buildings fingered
steely clouds while evening lingered ...
an atmosphere so purple, bleak, and grey
one might have said, 'It's like Buffet.'

"And then this evening, how nice it was,
the first snowfall
casting the city in strange chiaroscuro,
big, silent flakes —you know the type—
and afterwards the sloosh of traffic
whose tail lights ribboned red on pavements wet and black,
and later still—
the maple streets of yellow window light.

"And even now, as we walk this windswept street,
a plum-rubescent bruise swells in the southwest sky,
inflicted by
a steel mill that lies along the river's edge;
a twelve mile dragon who sleeps and fumes
along the river's edge having first devoured
a thousand dozen drudgers ... "

And I,
who know no why for our invention,

also keep keeping on by obscure intention;
and wonder what use words at all,
for how could I tell just how
those bells,
distant and out-of-tune,
just now, prod
some childhood bruise?—
And I wonder why I try.
And wonder, have I learned nothing along the way?

* * *

This forgotten edge of town
    —a labyrinth of shambled dwellings
where dilapidated shades can't hide
the naked bulbs within.
Our footsteps echo; a gust of wind
ransacks an alleyway, pirouettes, grins
    —flashing icicle teeth—
and vanishes on down the street;
something stirs in a sheltered corner;
brown weeds in a vacant lot poke through
an inch of newsprint snow, where shadow-like
against a broken wall of brick,
a coughing topcoat doubles, hacks, and spits;
then, in an icy freight train rush of wind,
a beer can rattles rattles rattles rattles rattles along the street;
this deserted street
where streetlights sometimes aren't
and partially burnt-out marquees mark
establishments among the ruins
in the dark
between the signs of EAT and BAR & GRILL

a warehouse stands in one-light gloom,
and as we pass at this late hour she reassures
there'll be no problem with the room.

* * *

Now, drawing the shades against the flashing
of some neon claim, I turn
and can't help note the question of it all;
I watch all but her necklace fall.
Then something said,
a nod of head, a certain smile
and for awhile
at least a little while upon the sheets ...

But even as I bend to meet
the turns I take,
I'm anxious to be on the straight again,
preparing for another bend.

A dim lamp lights the room
and casts the image of a chair
across the threadbare rug
to where a brass rail bed fits snug
against the further wall;
an out-of-season spider crawls
beneath a shelf;
beyond the dirty yellow light
a hunchbacked shadow fights itself.

Later, when all is sad and done,
and one by one
I pick my clothing from the floor,

she wants to know if there'll be more.
"Probably," I say,
not meaning it her way,
and by the door
she wants to know again
and when.

I recall as I descend the stair
her stare, level, over knees hugged white,
and even more, the sight
of naked toes that gripped a dingy mattress edge
     —I pause ... but no—
And on the empty street again,
amid a feathering of snow,
I turn my collar against the cold.

It was the same
and always and all it was not my aim.

THE TEMPERATURE OF LOVE

a sequence

The Temperature of Love

In a feathering of snow;

outside the apartment,
whose yellow windows
Scrabbled comfort;

in the cold shine
of a streetlight
through clicking branches—

the temperature of love!

• • •

Hot from the heat of her body,
the key
was more than I had ever hoped
to hold
of her warmth.

The Bruise

with the bruise that clouds
her white thigh   showing

not Botticelli's
but mine   standing in a tub

with hands not delicately placed
but calmly at the sides

with chestnut hair cut short
and eyes   cinnamon-to-ash

striking the saddest chord
in a melancholy mode   not Venus

Amy
clouding my reason

The Pearl

The sickness of the oyster
is the pearl.   Durrell

This nettling pang, this grain of sand,
with which I must cohabit this shell
till my luck runs out
is just my luck and calling;
a faith
to which I must adhere as the barnacle adheres
or this irritation and its fruit
are for nothing,
and I will have been wounded
for all the tides of the ocean
and to no avail.

The Compact

The compact mirror gave a dim, distorted view
of that which lay behind her
as she fixed her make-up
on the sidewalk of the wind-swept avenue.
For a moment,
I was not part of the geography overshadowed
by that Botticelli face marred
by the thin, white scar above one narrow eyebrow;

how I hated her
for her reflection.

The Egg & The Pearl

When the egg, the bond, we had
so painstakingly shaped
—cracked— and ran mucus
and pus through the fingers of my
astonishment, it was as though she had died—

And I walked the unreal streets
of midnight sun, rubbing
dim the braille of my dime
destiny in a pocket of indigo—

Till one morning, in the midst
of mourning, it dawned, with Damascan
brilliance, how I might minus
to plus my fortune —simple—

  pearl pearl a new belief
  around grief's insistent grit.

This symbol ** is used where double-spaces fall on page breaks.

An Offering, Mean and Poor

I am the flowering at the end of a long, bleak stem.

I am the flowering
   after the flickering flirtations
   of the neon, nylon nights,
   and the winter sidewalks
   past yellow window lights;

I am the flowering at the end
   of the ending nights of unending melancholy,
   nights of cigarettes and barroom folly;

I am the flowering
   after a certain pinprick dread
   tormented me down the narrow years,
   like a tiny bee about my head;

I am the flowering
   after the invalid shut the door
   on a room weary of an ever rearranged decor;

    (*I would mend my mind*)

   and after my brown-eyed mother's God frowned
   beyond belief —Jesus, was He ever friend—

and after the egg of one flesh cracked
   leaking mucus and pus
   through the fingers of my astonishment

**

    (though in a woman's love laugh,
    beyond an apartment wall,
    I found that one half of mankind was all
    the world to me)

  after all this—

     (I go on trying trying to thread
       a needle by candlelight)

          after all this and much untold,
I am the flowering at the end of a long, bleak stem,
a posy offered to you, Kathleen,
out of the effects of my days on this earth,
an offering, mean and poor,
offered for reasons obvious and obscure.

The Lesson

Where she lives in a room with a few things
I was a fool,
fool to wish comprehension
of an incomprehensible mathematics.

I should have accepted the calculus
of uncalculated love,
and the friendship of her body,
unconditionally;

I should not have asked
for the equations of time past,
should not have asked.

The Loft

There in the loft,
        where we had two mattresses
and between them
        a hurricane lantern,

I watched you sleep—saw
the grain of your hair flow
        dark
over the pillow and one white shoulder

laid bare by an errant quilt,
        a spill
of walnut over linen over almond;
        and heard

the wild wind ransacking
        the wastes of winter
in the edgeless black around us;
        heard it

rage around our parenthesis
of lantern light and love,
        our space capsule
between yesterday and tomorrow,

        our bubble (oblong) in a level,
I wished would never tilt.

After the End

Perhaps I felt the way a woman feels
who knows she is barren. I certainly felt
as if I had watched the world through windows,
as if I did not belong to the human race.

Slayed my dragon, though, by George.
Took him in the soft of the underbelly,
laid him out long as life.

But for all of that, the tail keeps sweeping
the distance, keeps on twitching like a snake's
that will switch till sundown.

What I want to know is, how long is this going
to go on—till sundown . . . my sundown?

PEDAL POINT

from:
Unworldly Wind

Pedal Point

The road winds

      down

           and

                down

                      through

    russet, wet and tattered woodland,

Windshield wipers bow & scrape, bow & scrape,

And serpentine the creek thrashes in its skintight gulch, having
    swallowed a storm

      overnight
      overnight

Grand schemes mostly tarnish, yet yesterday's Ys needs but a rub

    and a holler—

**

"Hwæt!"

And back she comes, her spires, her domes, her watery bells
       (burnished bronze in an ever lavender evening)—
While this other, darkly perceived, darkly persists—this

> *Dim of afternoon and snowfall-gray,*
> *Where in shadow of buttressed wall she comes,*
> *Stands with me—mute—on the first stone step of three*
> *Above a path that passes through winter-drifted hush*
> *Of churchyard monuments, to cross a footbridge into*
> *Wooded-darkness of winter woods beyond—*
> *The small stream trickling under ice—*
> *The silent snowflakes*
> > *falling*
> > > *falling . . .*

I woke!, sad of a wish for what there never was—

         · · ·

Down-shifting now, trav'ling fast over yellow leaves pasted to wet
       macadam (roller coaster stuff),
The rain-dripping woods on either hand,
The lasting lavender dusk of dream on my mind, and on
       the radi-♪ *o-o-o sweet baby* ♪—voice you'd love
       to sleep with,
And I am 3 decades back in Elyria, where evenings once settled on
       amber fields, like dusky lingerie still warm . . .
Where at the ragged edge of town waited Tate's Tavern and the
       almost nights of certain unlikelihoods, never ending . . .

         · · ·

The russet woods; Elyria; the dusk of dream; the lost city of Ys
　　　. . . amber, violet, rust motifs,
And like a dark pedal point, the agonies my steadfast father
　　　suffered, that for all my acquiescence, metaphysical,
　　　I know not what to think,
The mind adverts!

But *o-o-o* that radi-*o* voice, that curl of blue smoke, and the years
　　　touch thumb and finger—
And there's Syd, the very picture of a black face in negative, come
　　　to front his band at Tate's that Halloween, laughed our
　　　collective asses off—
And what might my father have made of my nights at Tate's?, out
　　　of his steady life and pasture ways　(I am uneasy that the
　　　dearly departed thumb our brains for lack of books),
And his faith and my faith, being what they are, the same end
　　　by means unreconcilably expressed

♪ ... *but o sweet baby* ... ♪

They don't mesh:　his kingdom a hillside acre; my trek into
　　　the orchid night . . .
His last act, to match new stone work with old, and each old
　　　stone hand selected from Penn's sylvan legacy—
　　　I remember, was there,
4 years old with a joy buzzer in my guts, knowing it to be
　　　a borrowed truck that had got its differential hung up
　　　on a mossy ledge . . .
Then some 18 odd years later, me again,

lone firefly pulsing through endless forest of unending night,
　　　ceaseless odyssey, epic eternal . . .

**

And now, the bottom of Thompson Hill Road and the old
    palomino: pensive old guy; hammock-slung and yellowing
    like ivory; constant as any old friend;

♪ *ol' pal o' mío* ♪

With back, rain-stained; and tail, lank to his fetlocks; he grazes
    lightly, the green October grass.

. . .

Coming along the valley road, the radio now an irritant: I punch
    punch punch the station settings, give Frank the finger
    ('that's life'), and twist it off,

And looking up—see! that the Halloween flare of the great
    pasture maple has guttered out—last night's winds, no
    doubt,

♪ *don't let Satan fff it out, this little light of mine* ♪

Devil be damned!

I sing of a siren and a sunken city—

    . . . Ellingtonian tones, city by Hammett, with lone
    nocturnal saxophone, or Mr. Eliot's violet hour
    transposed to Johnstown, Pennsylvania . . .

The black and purple emery of a certain evening gathers over level
    clean-edged roof lines (grainy like a newsprint photo, if
    you look intently)

And me a kid, aching for the imagined one night stands of an era
    gone, thinking the desolate streets I walk, a poetry, when
    over a café curtain—What?!

A barmaid intent on fixing a red red garter circling a round white
    thigh caught in a fishnet stocking, black; and me, a kid,
    taut and taunted, teased beyond reason . . .

That wonderful evening
    (barmaid, my ass)

That wonderful evening, so like that Ys-z city of perpetual purple
    twilight dreamed—but J'town, Steel Town, with its wine-
    stained sky . . .

        . . .

After 45 years in the mills, after 45 years a machinist, without
    the qualifying loss of a finger, so not a machinist after all,
    but still a hero, what the surgery did.

17 hours they labored and for what?

What Lugosi did to Karloff in "The Raven," 1935—though,
    in fact, a heinous accident enacted slow-motion on
    the surgeon's sterile plank, 1990.

Now farther along the valley, I see, in pelting rain, a half-a-
    hundred Guernseys, munching as they mosey northward
    toward the wooded hillside, its reds and golds subdued in
    the pelting rain, and think, 'he would have smiled at such
    a sight.'

        . . .

What the surgery did.

17 hours they labored, opened the head from behind the ear

forward, like a book cover, read the malaise and scraped the bone clean of the fatal thought; the censorship done, 'a closed book,' 'all sewed up,' leaving the knowledge of pain, unspeakable.

Yes. Unspeakable.

For a closed book doesn't speak, can't swallow, has a broken eye, the twisted face of a movie monster; but the mind clear, cognizant of the happened horror, and lucid to spell out home concerns on a clip board alphabet,

The least, the last I could do, draw him an alphabet large enough.

Inside my chest a scum bubble foul of grief swells, till one great 'SOB' bursts, having taken me unawares, as has so often happened this past year . . .

Can't afford to think on it.

Even a philosophy large enough to contain all the trees of an endless forest that holds in its whispery green-dusk all mysteries, cannot, or has not as yet, informed me what to think—

Branch after branch after branch as far as thought can reach, the Universe is as big as you think it is, and trying to think it 1 or 2 trees more, I think—

What if, lost, you came to a shack in the forest—found in the half-light beneath the leafy vaults where shone a beam of sunlight, a hermitage . . .

Found there, a hermit-sage. One like those marvelous saints of Ys—say, Guénolé, in all his ascetic excess

> (the brackish water; the few loaves twice
> a week, mixed with ashes; the praying right
> straight out for 7 hours, arms held level
> over gravity),

**

Oh wondrous excess set against such wickedness as Dahut
    princess of the Mary-Morgan sort—

"But Hey!
I can sing of waters what washed a town away . . . "

· · ·

JOHNSTOWN, MAY 31, 1889.
The approaching flood water was heard as a continuous
    thunder. My grandmother heard it.
Though only 5, remembered it.
Saw the second-story wall burst in as they clambered for the roof.

> It was a 40 foot wave that came on the town, that day.
> A rolling brow with a 'death mist' hanging over it.
> And before it, by a split second, a force of air
> knocking small frame structures flat. Now there's the
> grit of an American epic, having that needful national
> character of a people. 'Snatchy grabs' on the
> playground. Remember? A greed that grabbed a town
> away, complete, as a hand that scoops up marbles at
> the recess bell, or dice (after a bad throw for 'us').
> And no one called to make an account. Yes,

I've all that in my veins, and Ys I know.

Can I do it?—

Sing
    (in long alliterative lines of longing)
      steeples and spires into being,

Whoop the warp of watery bells into being,
Call up towers and domes and castles,
From emerald waters till high over all,
Higher than the highest pinnacle of all,
Cry the pewter castle of the pagan princess,
Cry the Korrigans castle, grandeur against God
By the pagan princess, wild unruly Dahut—

Can I do it?

Say the several sylvan saints of Quimper,
Shout the sieges of Grandlon, and sorrows whisper,
Bellow the grief and speak the grievance,
Sing the polyphony of flaw and treachery
To the last speck of the splendor lost . . . ?

And still farther along the valley road, the all Summer summer-
long baseball field in rain.

. . .

Last Spring, across this same faded field, a large smoke plume
hooked and flowed up river, a river itself, turning quite
blue as it thinned amid the hillside trees, of the winter
rusted, rested woods . . .

Last Spring, on an apple bough, a fat-backed bird turned
sideways—revealing his identity—and the next day two
more of his kind eyed me from a crocus lawn. 'An
infestation of robins!' I thought, and thought,

'He always saw the year's first robin' (though allowed as how
that February robin had likely wintered over).

He could look down, anytime-anywhere, and find a four-leafed
clover, it didn't take him long, and then it came to me
as it comes to me now, that I will always see the first

Spring robin first, find the four-leafed clovers . . .
And now ahead of me, the town of Colrain nestled at the base
of the mountain, with its old brick church: blue-roofed,
white steeple aslant . . .

. . .

Was it just two years ago, Christmas, that we came early through
the valley, the air clear and cold, and there at
the mountain's base the little town of Colrain?
How still we saw thee, in the morning light,
With a kinked plume of smoke moveless over each and every red
brick chimney (a greeting card picture if there ever was
one),
And in the house beneath each smoke-?ed roof, Christmas, about
to happen to each excited boy and girl, always anew since
the advent of this unique event—
Then up the mountain we went on our way to a Boston Christmas,
that winter morning, yes, two years ago—

. . .

Today, down-shifting to take the mountain (the windshield wipers
bowing & scraping),
The subdued reds and golds of the mountain trees up and ahead,
My thoughts in shades of amber dusk, and dusk of dream;
in shades of Ys, and lone nocturnal saxophones . . . amber,
violet, bronze, or rouge motifs—
And underneath it all . . .

The grim incessant drone of a grave insistent tone

PART TWO

from:

Adrift

selections from: Blue Night

this moonless night
this hush
of falling snow
by lamplight
your five haiku

for Yasuko Fukumi

I stick with the
weather

the erotic jive
in her eyes

    shuts
    down

selling flowers,
she wears
nothing but
the briefest briefs
beneath her dress

lovely to see,

but her snippy way
withers
my fine bouquet
of notions

in his tree house,
red as the rose
that newly sprung
this June,
he blooms with shame

having blurted out
his secret

picking up the dime
from the sidewalk
she shows the bird nest
between her breasts
– and then her beard

along the winter streets,
the lifeless streets
of yellow window lights
and leafless trees, I pass
– a click of cleats

her skirt brightens
in the sunlight at the door
quick! quick!
her scissor shadow
cuts me through

on the terrace

under the stars
we talk

the rub of wind
my velvet

along
the narrow sidewalk
as two lovers pass me
the snag
of a privet on my sleeve

"okay! okay! he's everything a woman wants.
now what's for supper?"
                              the petals
of yesterday's rose lie around the vase

*"He never meant a thing to me,
honest."*

across the inlet
a row
of shingled houses

the dishwater slosh of the sea

"... and don't expect me back"

morning now
smoke from a neighbor's chimney

saw grass
showing
the wind's way

we all have our secret selves,
but to hear it
on the twisted sheets of love –
my whole body
a stubbed finger

the chickadee
sits
on a phone line
its talons
like
two spiders
dancing on
its belly

frost-stars on
the windshield

at the bus stop,
two friends
speak clouds

icy roads
controlling the car with prayer & rectum

home at last

the cat sniffs and sniffs
the damage

the car
more hurt
than was the bear

from a 19th century Yankee diary

Killed my hog.
Broke my heart.
Went to work.

beyond the window, a boney dump*

each classroom
heated by a wood furnace

in summer
from the mine's maw
cool scary air

*slag heap

Where a Flower Should Be

A thought dwelt on
can only grow –

and a weed is a bad thought
where a flower should be.

A thought dwelt on
is a thought given water,

but a weed deprived of water
withers away.

Learning to Float on Your Back

> You believe
> it can be done, yes,
>
> that the water
> will support you, certainly,
>
> but
> there is a moment
>
> when you must finally relax
> and let it happen –
>
> this is called
> Knowing.

reality
is what you think it is
and facts are faceted

pick a glint pleasing
to your eye

think what you want

thinking
about Rodin's *The Thinker* –
thinking,

mind
over
matter matters

or nothing matters

tomorrow
is the best day yet,

giving us hope
and other
unusable tools

for today's
jury-rigged work

the fountain nude
forever bent
to pluck a bronze flower
think of it
and revel in uncertainty

nice to be
a museum piece –
bronze knockers
and crotch, both
burnished by secret hands

also on display that day
at The Museum of Modern Art
an anonymous print:
medium;
lipstick on tissue

the radiators bang

cod liver oil washed down
by fresh squeezed orange juice

he sits by the oven
warm on one side
shivering on the left

Saturday morning

*"you kids stop bouncing around,
you'll make the dough fall"*

button button
who's got
the button

somehow

on the way
to Aunt Alice's

the center
of the cherry pie
disappeared

biting the head off

the gingerbread man first,
I tell my 5 yr. old

that it's more humane
and
part of our oral tradition

Thanksgiving Day

candles and wine
a 3 lb. turkey

snow falling
through maple branches
a man and a woman . . .

carolers

a cloud before
each oval mouth

and toes so cold
the rum can't
rouse them

raspberry picking

as she turns to me
a swift cloud shadows her face

like
forgotten
sorrow

family barbecue

burnt offerings
the *'chock'* of
croquet balls

old,
her eyesight gone
she sits apart

faintly smiling

his clothes to charity

unpacking the suitcases
of the vacation no longer awaited

finding
the Valentine meant
for today

a few friends gather

mulled wine
the sweets of sophistry

after the last guest leaves
standing under
the starry sky

in a pool of lamplight   my pensive art

under a gunmetal sky
the goldenrod's strong yellow

mystique is where you make it so

a door
waits
to be opened

Midnight and the mind meanders ... memory
and imagination – nation enough for odyssey . . .

Up above this world of care,
Han-Shan, old hand at solitaire.

Clay Tablets

all these years
dropping pebbles into a well
the small splash
of a poem's acceptance
then silence

yes, yes
it's the work that matters
not fame
still
I don't write for a wastebasket

for posterity
I suggest publishing
on clay tablets
your local landfill
as good a depository as any

the stir of curtains
on a clover scented evening . . .

in my fingers
the feel of his logic –
Johann Sebastian Bach

roses
and wrought iron fences

the novel long deferred
memory
without meaning

only grass
where the homestead stood

even here
I am far
from home

overnight a winter wonderland

chickadees flit from branch to earth –
feed, squabble, and return to branch

only
to be
reborn

                              don't care much

                              for rasping dogmas
                              or chiseled tenets

                              my way
                              more like the wind
                              in the willows

the 10,000 things

a hidden path
leads into the mountains

in a hut
the old poet lives
alone   alone

wineshop girls

quarreling
as they pretty and prepare

and did you find,
Tzu Yeh,
your gold orchid friend

Atlantic crossing

three days without sight of land
yet looking up tonight

a nugget
of
real estate

"*hast du Feuer?*"

shying away
she leaves her sly smile
but not her name

where she stood
a twist of blue smoke

Piazza San Marco

a pigeon rides my head
for several steps

I feel
– how shall I say –
blessed

museum tour

appearing and reappearing
braless in t-shirt

valued at more
than all the naked
statues

you're gone

the rain rivulets down
our café window

how to say it?
Venus de Milo handcuffed
to a museum mind

a streetlamp

casting a path over snow-melt
where five pines stand

that's all it takes
one moment an insomniac
the next a tourist in Færy

newly anointed

a shadowy figure in thin muslin
her braceleted arms raised

of man's first dawn
bison on cave walls
shards & dust

        in the market place

        dust and dung
        a fly riding the piper's finger

        threading the crowd
        a woman in white
        magical as a unicorn

urban midnight

in a pool of yellow lamplight
his craft or sullen art*

after long illness
an el Greco
in the garret window

*Dylan Thomas – paraphrased

a room
and a means of livelihood

beholden to no one
and
the boarding house lady
I'll never forget

hitch-hiking   a coal truck stops

six miles farther on
an invite for coffee

in the kitchen
chickens and a fridge full
of Schlitz

mission house rules

in by nine, sober & a shower
– come morning,

coffee & oatmeal
never tasted
so good

the bike clocked at 135 mph

midnight and flatland in all directions
one stone and it's over

Lorain to Oberlin
15 miles   7 minutes
me & Cyd

            rainy night outside Ray's

            blue neon gleams
            on the wet parking lot

            it happens
            and he's down and dead
            justlikethat

miles davis & blue lights

at this hour
some of the girls dance topless

at this hour
a spider slowly
yo-yos

spring breezes open nightgowns

somewhere
in the kiss of dawn
a ruby explosion
loud
to no man's eye

an impossible math this
but over the years
inch by inch
how many miles
of sex?

always

it may be
the shadow of
a hedge
or the dusk of
a tool shed
or the darkness
surrounding
a party
but whatever else
it may be
it is always
touch and go
for lovers

after the nights

of pills
and
prayers
and
sad songs – you,

my Androcles

after
the many sunsets
viewed

through an ashen blur
of migraine

only the sunsets now,

as if there'd been
no blur

The Room Behind

Always conscious
of the room behind,

and its too familiar
furniture, and

the weary
rearrangements of

its too familiar
furniture,

I have watched the world
through windows.

Epilogue

This Life Without Sub-titles

fall colors   eyeglasses
on an eyeless styrofoam head
– all this behind glass,
          and something antique
          about the gilt leaves of the locust

rated R for 'brief nudity'
one lousy unclothed mannikin
I kid you not
          my first inflatable girlfriend,
          remembering her seamy side

always on the outside
looking in
          this life without sub-titles
          no better than
          a peeping Tom's

a band of gold or handcuffs,
what difference?
'I've seen it all' says Tom
          clearly
          there's more here than meets the eye

vacant store front
graven in dust
a two-word audacity
        the blurting finger having writ
        rubs grit on a denimed thigh

when two raindrop rivulets
mmeeeett
one drinks the other –
        never knowing which side you're on,
        the trouble with windows

the Waterford vase
on display
a spray of blue asters
        after the shock of eyes that cease to see
        – wildflowers in profusion

a calico curled
in the bookshop window
        between two snowflakes
        'a spill of apples'
        the surprise of seeing the book we made

from:

THIS HUNGER, TISSUE-THIN

new & selected tanka 1995 - 2005

again tonight
along the color-ribboned river
I feel its frail insistence –
this hunger, tissue-thin
behind my breastbone

hearing your fame on the radio,
I go walking streets of leaves –
longing to see you,
I ache,
having no success to speak of

looking down
on that distant page
of meadow –

a railroad train straight as a sentence
and I too mountain high to read its noise

along the river
where trees are glad with leaflets,
she had to tell me –
later, pitched across the hotel bed,
I wept

a drizzly day,
with yellow leaves pasted
to wet black pavement -
returning the library books
she left behind . . .

the girl
could have done better
in White River Junction
than run into my arms
and the set-
        ting
            sun

Rorschach treescape
and moon fleeced clouds . . .
how unlikely,
against a yellow windowshade,
this perfect female profile

when I think
that we may never
meet again . . .
this hillside of aspens
endlessly fluttering

I've come again
to this oak-gripped bank,
who knows why? –
recalling our last time here,
I watch a red leaf drift out of sight

standing in the green-dusk
of the woods looking out –
how bright the meadow . . .
how odd this reluctance
to step into brilliance

in maple shade,
trying
to match mind
to pond, thoughts
to trout

at twilight the flame
in the bush is candlelight
caught by the window –
nothing more, nothing less
  – is what you make of it

frost-stars on the window,
hills in the purple distance . . .
if I thought
it'd do some good I'd rave
of things invisible to see

a thistledown floats
over grass and Queen Anne's lace
this yellow afternoon . . .
and what have I to do
with tumultuous times?

around the campfire
singing with the others,
I flick an unworthy thought
from my mind –
a spark from my sleeve

streetlights
illume the maples
from within . . .
was it so much, my love,
to expect the truth?

the tilt
of her head to undo
an earring –
fortresses crumble into
winter moonlight

"I couldn't help myself"
that's what she said,
and all this long day's journey into night
　　imagination
　　an intolerable jingle

at the window,
after our long night, raindrops dripping
through copper leaves –
say what you like,
there's no one truth in such matters

sweet scent of lilacs
I watch a bee question cluster
after cluster –
this endless ache for intimacy
what good is it?

the dawn's gray effusion grieves
for lack of color,
lack of warmth –
all I know of love
wouldn't fill a sonnet

this long sidewalk
with its clatter of penny-brown
oak leaves –
   all my good days
   faded to illegibility

embroidering & embroidering –
over the years
the best of her creativity
spent
on an old affair

in the night-fog
a yellow bruise
where the streetlight was –
any truth is better
than indefinite doubt

still angry,
I hear an acorn
bouncing down
the branches of the oak –
my fist flowers to catch it

looking up, I gaze
at the faded reds and golds
of an autumn hillside –
the story in the old tapestry
not at all what I remembered

at the chapel window
the wind-stirred bittersweet . . .
lately,
and I don't know why,
great age seems unnecessary

in eternity
how can it matter much
but still
that dim December afternoon
I might have been there

these first cool nights
a neighbor burns apple wood . . .
it's not so much memory
that comes wafting back
        as a trace of legend

just walking sidewalks,
a stranger
in a strange town,
when a child from his lawn
says "hello"

lonely
in my haste to nowhere
in particular
a sidewalk robin
gives me the eye

I'm just saying
how good it is to see her
when suddenly
she sticks out her tongue –
catches a snowflake

on the station platform
in a feathering of snow
I see her first –
in my chest
a stop-motion rose . o p e n i n g

having run out
of propane
we go to bed early –
her warmth the length of me
this winter night

geraniums in a windowbox,
a young wife leaning out
to tend them –
        when did my heart
        become a fist?

here where the river
is wide and smooth
and red leaves drift by slowly –
here ... remembering when
the dream was clear

touch ... touch ...
the skipping stone hits
the farther bank . . .
suddenly I am old
and understand nothing

the river snakes
across the plain into
the blue distance –
it's not so much a fear of what's to come
as of nothing left to do

on the kitchen table
daisies
in a green bottle
all I need
everything I want

since morning
3 pears on a green plate are 2 –
alone
I craft these wintry lines,
the afternoon silent as granite

a dozen
roses are a dozen
roses,
but one rose
is a friend

lined with locust trees
a small street I love
its main event a pastry shop
and the sparrows
the small quick sparrows

in the light
of the hurricane lantern,
the walking stick
by the cabin door –
friend enough this winter night

back home
walking with a favorite uncle
toward the stream's source –
no longer a common alphabet
to spell our affection

the war ended,
he brought home from the Isle of Capri
a 'real' cameo
imagine its enchantment
there on the oil cloth table top

heads or tails?
well if it's heads, there you have her
Mrs. Wallace Stevens
in bas-relief
and still only a dime

the blue,
the piercing blue of Sirius.
more you will never share
the nuances are mute
– art's first hard lesson

using the wind,
by allowing the wind
full play –
this butterfly, not much more
than a folded piece of paper

red as sunrise
tOmatOes alOng the windOwsill
   too many shadows
   too much reflection
time for something plump in the hand

first light
and again I'm brewing coffee –
like an ant
on a moebius strip
this dailiness

for fifty years
through all the weathers
of the mind,
I have loved the world with my eye
. . . if nothing else, that

ever a pebble
in my shoe
since that one false step
on the beach
at Marblehead

walking
the railroad tracks
alone –
more and more we live
our parallel lives

what delighted me most
now leaving me
    petal
    by
    petal

tanka sequences

SOMETHING TO REALIZE

I look up from her letter,
my worst fear realized,
just in time to see
a goldfinch leave
the thistle's purple bloom

it's something
to realize you're nothing
to somebody else –
      blue smoke rising
      from a farther hill . . .

a drizzly day,
with yellow leaves pasted
to wet black pavement –
returning the library books
she left behind

bittersweet in such plenty,
an orange-and-yellow mist
that wants telling . . .
if she will not answer my letters,
          if she *will* not

along the winter streets,
the lifeless streets
of yellow window lights
and leafless trees, I pass
        – a click of cleats

* * *

Hidden In Brush

hidden in brush
not noticed till now,
the doe –
eyes meet eyes till neck folds
and body vanishes

the cat
sniffs and sniffs
the damage –
the car more hurt
than was the bear

in the face
of the approaching pedestrian
I see something,
something to wince about –
then hear the crash behind me

only five years,
and she's lost her face
to flesh! –
the mystique gutters,
infatuation dies

the dawn's gray effusion grieves
for lack of color,
lack of warmth –
all I know of love
wouldn't fill a sonnet

* * *

LEAFLESS IT STANDS

leafless it stands,
wrought iron against a washed-out sky –
over the gnar
of the chainsaw I shout
"that one stays, it's sculpture now"

in a muslin of rain
the October leaves subdued
the pumpkins shiny
a gunshot in the woods
shatters the quiet

waking to a certain hush
I know what to expect
yesterday's world
reduced to the mere suggestion
of a charcoal sketch

ditched car
the crunch of snow underfoot
all that last mile home
bleak branches
strung with constellations

udders full
the cows turn westward
in the gathering dusk
a radio in the barn
issues the news

the old cow
hikes her pump handle
and lets splash –
I smile, remembering
my grandfather's laugh

* * *

Two for Li Po

bleak branches
strung with constellations
   – Colrain and now –
imagine - the same geography
once extolled by Li Po

that Li Po, drunk,
leaned over the boat's side
to embrace the moon
and drowned . . . ?
sure, I believe it

        * * *

My Helplessness

in the park
a mockingbird holds forth
feeling fetal again
only skirt fever
keeps me erect

magnolia petals
cluttered around the ruins
of a sundial –
my helplessness
before a woman in tears

discussing plans
for the annual fund raiser –
painfully aware
that beneath the white dress
there's a woman

so foxy
the new clerk at the gift shop –
watching now
the river slip beneath the bridge
I'm in no hurry to go home

trying to look her in
the eye as she explains
the Egyptian mummy –
her nipple-ring outlined beneath
the museum t-shirt

level clean-edged roof lines
against an evening sky
the tune of an era gone
my long-legged, lean and lovely,
where are you now?

* * *

ORDINARY MOMENTS

night of heavy snow.
back from the barn by flashlight
footsteps already blurred –
in the window
the red-tipped electric candle

Auld Lang Syne
under a starry sky
sparks from a hilltop bonfire
what's done is done
and some things best forgotten

first light
and again I'm brewing coffee –
like an ant
on a moebius strip
this dailiness

out of a pearly sky
a few snowflakes fall
through black branches –
utter silence . . .
but for a woodpecker at work

* * *

New Territory

while I slept
it snowed
and a tree fell
old age
uncertain as a winter road

some things
are never going to happen again
others
never again, that way,
and still others, never

having entered new territory
– a tundra at dusk –
I await,
anxious and somewhat fearful,
the undefined adventure

* * *

The Way of Things

in the grey distance
the line between sky and hillscape,
barely discernible –
without faulting the facts
memoir becomes legend

standing among stately pines
disgraced and alone in my outcast state
yet always,
always an integral part
of the universe

to pick up the beach
grain by grain, how long?
in eternity
no time at all, I think –
the endless hour glass trickles trickles

first light
morphing into shadowless dawn
perfect stillness
what I am I am
right here   right now

* * *

from:

OUTER EDGES

a collection of tanka

on my back
on a bed
in a bed & breakfast –
my dime destiny
mapped on a cracked ceiling

trying trying
to get hold of – not the hat,
wind-tumbled down the street,
but
my last earthly desire

to sculpt a destiny
or simply squeeze
the clay
and take what comes
?

at the gallery entrance
she pauses
all hip & lipstick –
a nail driven through
a calendar date

the sound of the siren
is as red
as your lips closing over
the blind white
of the hard boiled egg

in the streetlight
the red of her paisley dress purples
as do her lips –
lips that are saying
something that makes me blue

the mannequin's skirt flaps open
& open & o' how
this spring breeze taunts
recalling the quick nuptials
of amber afternoons & neon nights

in my mind's eye
I can see her in a thong &—& nothing . . .
my god!
so this is the life of the mind
who'd have thought

at the checkout
reading all
the tabloid headlines –
    the curse
    of literacy

talking with three guys
the co-ed shields herself
with a book –
          imagine,
Shelley guarding her chastity

inside the grape arbor,
shadowed-patterns where her blouse
lies open –
the purple fruit
wants tasted

his hand
at the moment of birth
a leaflet
his fate, his character
a decisive ideogram

hands that held
this family Bible held reins,
spun wool, penned,
on yellowed fly-leaves,
these brown and faded names

no one left
to tell again the family stories,
the farm stories,
and how the great poet came to sit
in the chair I sit in now

gas flames rise
from fake logs,

the tribe's
story teller,

a Kindle

while I wait
to be served, I devise a story
in the willowware –
we've each of us our beliefs
and our own supporting evidence

that we can live on finer
& finer energy fields –
sure, why not?
if you can believe this world
you can believe any world

Dec. 24th - 25th

falling snow
past streetlights holiday
the parking lot –
at Starbucks an answer
from tomorrow's Toyko

wide snow,
all else perpendicular – the tall trees,
the icicles off the porch eve –
    and I, too, am upright
    in my solitude

by lantern light
stacking pennies
five deep
& five deep –
waiting out the storm

Nefertiti –
was there ever such a woman?
what I wouldn't give
to stand in her aura,
know what she thought of her world

in wet sand
the chain
of her elegant footsteps
end
midway to nowhere

always fascinated by
that last half-inch in the long crawl
of evolution
where mankind straightens
to step out of the picture

eons ago
an Eocene fish got buried in mud –
now framed
on my stairway wall
its fossiled fame

the sizzle
of crickets
tightens –
something about this mountain night
remembers ancient seas

glint
of braceleted arms, body
maddered by firelight –
I wake! to a trace
of goat and sandalwood

this past August,
all at once, the abuse of a decade
condensed into a bullet –
there's a house for sale
in our neighborhood

dusk
and the day lily all but done
    no one
    a statistic
    but once

I conjure our river bank
but it morphs,
it jungles
and the Rousseau-animals emerge –
those eyes! our sudden nakedness!

the sea-green pool
in the woodland river –
after 30 years and all
the great capitals of the world,
the sea-green pool

lying
under stars
becoming
a wide slow
river

monologues
with tome-tombed men

1
hang it all Browning,
it could almost be mine,
your *Andrea del Sarto*.[1]
his impossible love
and the greats known by him

[1] a paraphrase from A Draft of XXX Cantos; II,
by Erza Pound

2
Langland,[2]
when writing your great Vision
in Chaucer's London
you could not have envisioned this –
your words on my monitor tonight

— 2a
though six centuries sundered,
I find us fused by a common guilt
     verse
     vs.
     wage-work

— 2b
quoting, you wrote
"the laborer is worth his hire"
tell me about it! –
     still, my needs are met
     and my wants somewhat

[2] William Langland, 14th century author of
The Vision of Piers Plowman

3
and you, the sage of Concord [3]
       sane, credible, astute –
a common man
wild
in your own quiet way

    — 3a
mornings you wrote
afternoons hoed
took late walks to the Pond –yes,
but those lamplit conversations . . . o,
to have been a fly on your wall

    — 3b
trust thyself – your message
or as Campbell phrased it,
follow your bliss –
well I have,
guilt and lies not withstanding

[3] Ralph Waldo Emerson

4

Han Shan,[4] like you,
I never thought it'd end this way –
    you 'neath your pine
    me, my sumac,
our red dust days gone with the wind

5

Issa,[5]
where have I gone wrong? –
    indifferent to housework
    kindly to insects,
but revered –?   not at all

postscript:

not surprising, is it?, that more
and more, as each old friend ends
his or her grave march,
I hold endless monologues
with tome-tombed men

[4] 9th century Chinese Taoist poet, aka 'Cold Mountain'
[5] Kobayashi Issa, one of the four Japanese haiku masters

IN AN UPSTAIRS ROOM

60 cherita

*

selected and sequenced by ai li

spring breeze

a mannequin's skirt
flapping

that's all
it
takes

out of the blue

and without a word
she packed and left –

the locusts were buzzing
and the old dog lay
in the dusty drive

whiskey

and the Saturday night streets
of walking

touch-
me-
nots

in morning sunlight

strict as a sapling ash
she pours

a bucket of water
over
her nakedness

back & forth

we mirror one another
in the doorway

can it be?
a permanent
relationship . . .

sunset after sunset

these solitary walks
this ache to tell

the fiery furnace
closes and leaves me
to my dusk

against the white wall

her once full shadow now
a brushstroke

I focus on her voice
to remember
who she is

on a balcony

with a green bench
and an icon above it,

an old man smoking –
a fig
of his former self

after twenty years, again the room

the room my son
has rented unbeknownst

the room where I woke
to a carpet of spiders
that weren't

hoarfrost

10,000 apple drops
lie in the untended orchard

in the kitchen
a floor board
chirps

power outage

no candles
can't find the flashlight

the copper tea kettle
lit
by a ring of blue flame

the others have gone to town

my buddy's wife
dressed only in her loveliness

and no one need know
says
her smile

midnight

you phone from another hemisphere
to say you're through with him –

a black widow
stands
on the ceiling

wind & owls

and night like a shawl
drawn round my shoulders

if dawn
never came
I wouldn't mind

from my window

stitching past a row of trees
she is walking to town

down the stairs
two at a time
we meet ! by accident

beneath that smile

fingers
toying a button

the typo
on the tip
of my tongue

we went back in the woods

to where the old trolley tracks
went through

and that's were
we found him,
the crows had got his nose

you leaned

against me
and neither of us

moved
for the longest
time

for a moment

the bloom and the bee were one,
what happened next

let's
just call it
youth

working the grill

you should have seen his face
when the cops walked in

drugs
and underage videos
in an upstairs room

tangled sheets

tainting the walls
a neon's pulse

by the window
the glow
of a cigarette

cruel words

viewing the moon together
though 500 miles apart

the inadequacy
of long-stemmed
roses

the moon path laps her toes

across the lake   faint lights
bits and pieces of party noise

on the beach behind her
the shredded
letter

so that was that

now, breaking a dry stem
into bits

watching
the river
flow

October sunlight

hearing her love-laugh
from another room

staring at a knot-hole
in the red oak
flooring

death and distant thunder

the question
I dare not ask

a spring breeze fingers
a
hemline

flies, chickens & dog

while 3 drunk buddies fix the car,
she stands at the screendoor

bare breasted
diet coke in hand
watching

summer heat

on the porchsteps
9 red toenails, 1 to paint

young though she is
she's already a few
good secrets

it's her wedding tomorrow

she comes to me in the night
saying

*"this
will have to last
for a long time"*

after seeing you off

taking the path along
the canal

a rustle of
leaves
underfoot

if I'd the money

I'd move to the city
do drugs & fast women

&
squander
the rest

"light?"

in the casino where she stood
a twist of blue smoke

sleuthing her through
the sun-bleached streets
! seeing her nowhere

the door blows open

and the candles gutter
– the Ouija board

has just
spelt
d e a t h   h u r t s

all night with closed eyes

the ventriloquist's dummy lies
in its velvet box

for the first time
the muted many
dream their voices

so

tired
today

I could
take
root

will I outlive

this
economy size bottle

of vitamins?
that
is the question

henge

under a blue sky
buttercups slope away to the sea

a long way from here
the headstone
awaiting me

the eternal flame

blow it out
and the universe quits

who's to say there isn't
an eternal
match

granite

the
spacious

sound
of
nothing

on a sunlit rock

a passive pet
a corpse

the butterfly
whose wings in death are fixed
for flight

threading her way

through the crowd, the missing piece
to my jig-saw destiny

gone
as soon as
seen

following the path

out of the woods to a sudden
meadow, ravine and

wall of red autumn
right up
to heaven

apples float

and
muddy water clears

if
left
alone

seeing you again

and so much of you
in your string bikini

evening's wild colors
flung
on sky and water

alone at home

and nothing
needs doing

at the window
rain
a gust of leaves

overnight

a dusting of snow . . .
the many tracks of many creatures,

a Rosetta stone
of rural
nightlife

lightning whitens the room,

naked
at the window

your afterimage
a ghostly
daguerreotype

silently in a snapshot

you are saying something
and look wonderful saying it

the fall leaves are gray
and your smile
is forever

mid-afternoon

the heat packaged smell of asphalt
weeds and grass –

too straight,
too narrow,
this heartland road

for rent
a cliffside cottage

sumacs jungle the property

here I could be
a Ryōkan or
a Han Shan

teasing the mirror, she strips

not wanting to waste
the few good years she sees

in the study below
her scholar husband
living a life of braille

she knew

but didn't know quite
why the many eyes caressed her

in a white skirt
with
the sun behind her

at dusk

through sparse
& snow laden pines

boot tracks
enter
the woods

trapped

in the patina
of a 60-watt parlor

sipping tea and
smiling politely – the hypnotic
drone of decay

sudden downpour

in a church portal we wait
talking of Egyptology - me,

trying not to notice
the sodden cling
of her dress

she turns from the moonlit window

her breasts
cradled in her arms

and how I ask
are we to be
just friends?

festival lights

holding hands with a stranger
along the red-ribboned river

somewhere the faint bells
of a sunken city
under sea-green waves

crossing the churchyard in winter

on a headstone
her name   yet not her name

the electric instant
before
I hurry on

o, to watch

her cross the river's
pebbly stones again

again
to hear
her naked laugh

a table set for two – a roast in the oven

the phone rings
in a white dress she goes out

whether by choice
or chance – she steps
into traffic

from:

THE COLORS OF ASH

new and selected tanka & cherita

my life
at the violet edge of day

no second draft

fears of
the dark walk
with me

at first light

before the crack
of dawn

the crack
of an egg
on the skillet's rim

a grey

half-lidded
morning

the toast jumps
and I
jump

in
the sugar bowl

the ants
are having the time
of their life

– let them

putting out
kibble
for the feral cat
snow
on every branch

pigeons in a park

I feed them
and feed them

old humiliations
bob and coo
around me

so much
depends

on the busker

singing
a give away
interval

the song writer
with little melody
before him

dreaming
of silent pianos

in dim & dusty rooms

November sunlight
slants
through the window

a chess board waits

with only
a few moves left

old men

rake
leaves

winter it out
in
narrow beds

while I was ill

blossoms
came out

fields
were
plowed

thinking what
the surgeon does
when he opens up a chest –
thinking what
a timid life I've led

e x t e n d i n g his lifeline with a scalpel

we arrived

and there were his ashes
in an urn

after the service
we shopped
for cheese & wine

sharing
fruit cocktail
and table

we give
each other space

the yellow-jacket
and I

there's little to do here
but sip espresso
and watch the afternoon

I read much of the night

don't forget
to water the coleus

dawn comes

with its egg yolk insistence
mourning doves & duty . . .

the ceaseless monologue
kicks in
my unrecorded long-song

countless syllables

and still
and still

I've not
explained
myself

this creek

torrential in spring
a trickle now

all the things
in me
that wanted voice

long winter night

the scurry of
a squirrel in the walls

if I could capture just
one hour of my hectic mind
in a book . . .

all eight legs
of me

still
trying, trying
to get out

of the sink

skirting

the wrenched
geometry

cast

by the cabin's
yellow
window-light

a fox passes
on silent paws

a squeal

in
the orchard

life
feeds on
life

"to bring in
another cat

to sleep
on her couch
so soon

it'd be adultery"

caught kissing

her dog
on the lips she laughs

pasture roses bloom
along the path
above the beach

a gust of yellow leaves
cross the porch
the kitten's head turns
every which way
trying to see them all

tumbling
out of nowhere

a bronze leaf
lands
at my feet

the puzzle of omens

at the check-out,

her bewitching scent
woodsy-dark and pagan

some mother's son
tries to join
a coven

every bonfire
ceremony and ritual

ghost stories & marshmallows

as night owls
haunt
the woods

the river, autumnal & slow

we share with two strangers
the wide-winged heron's flight

later,
coffee & crumb cake
just you and me

white cup

lipstick stained
& empty

coins
strewn on a café table

Sapphic fragments
taunt my mind

our fingers
touch

the small
arithmetic
of

coins

coffee
&
conversation

always
my back

to the wall

this time, she tells me,

she's telling the truth –
between us

I watch the struggle
of a wasp drowning
in peach juice

she leaves in haste

she has to meet a *'friend'*
alone now,
I take up palette and brush

for that inexplicable
second caress

like
foreplay

photo

shopping
your
pics

four panes of darkness

the old house shifts
and creaks in the winter cold

on the table
a still life ready-made
for brush and oil

family in bed

and term papers graded
he steps, without hope,

into the snowy night
to see her
bedroom window lit

with twisted sheets
wet between her legs,
she wakes
from a dream by Bosch –
the angst of half-remembered pleasures

amid the shards of a nightmare i stand
empty handed   mute

scandal, disaster,
rumors of war . . .

a fly

wrings its hands,
eats cake,
wrings its hands

it's the little things

that tip me over
the edge

the spilled milk
the damaged flower
the lost kitten

a dusting

of snow tramped
into lace
by tiny talons

the taste
of woodsmoke

in the black of night

in my mind's ear
the galloping thump of paw pads

the ghost
of a dog
sorely missed

"give it up, Tansy,

it's not going to fall off the limb
just because your canines are showing"

well,
the chipmunk
did fall

your town-raised
Sheltie took in

our donkeys
and our llama
with equanimity,

but the cows –

the cows
were a suspension
of reality

a shallow swale
of old leaves
undulating

no –

hundreds of robins
just arrived

herbal tea & Chaurasia

how they arc & dip & dart
in little bursts

the chickadees
that feed
in the drive

trying to coax
the renegades home
with a bucket of oats –
daft on fermented windfalls
the cows, having none of it

one bite
of sugar pie

and I'm back

in that
oilcloth
kitchen

coal and steel
and the grit
that goes with them –
dandelion
was not a delicacy

somewhere
between Dickens
and Pynchon
the Rockwell days
of my dad

in the old photo
beside
his pretty wife

he looks so happy
in black & white

the colors of ash

from:

THE HORIZON
WAITS

selected tanka, cherita, haiku
& short free form

first light

and again
I'm brewing coffee

like an ant
on a moebius strip
this dailiness

on my way
to tell sad news

I pause

where a freshet
floods
a patch of violets

we did what we could

read their letters,
figured their taxes
good neighbors they

now just a cellar hole
and the lilacs in spring

home

just as the first raindrops
stain the sidewalk

tiger-lilies
by
the doorstep

stargazing

I know
how

stop-signs
get
peppered

it nags, but

damn it, all I want
is to stand on the porch

and watch
the red leaves
fall

he was
a quiet man
so a few

heartfelt
words

spoke volumes

tearoom chatter
&
late night thoughts

little by little
the old poet

leaking into eternity

those garret trysts

now coffee
and conversation suffice

reading lips
across
the clattering café

a perfect female profile

and my body sobs
as slowly

slowly
I fade into
spirit

the night is for the young
and for the solitaires
and I have been both –

soon, I will step into
the midnight forest,

become owl

fossilized

in the library book,
a mosquito

that ruddy stain
some reader's
DNA

the envelope
contained

a card, a photo,
a request for an autograph
and one

long blond hair

as the water skier lets go
    slows &
            sinks, so
this epilogue
to a bookman's long career

inch by inch
the inch-worm goes
by the book

the coreid bug,
antique, slow & mechanical –
a thought escaped
from the mind of Jules Verne
still walking

clutching violets

a woman in stilettos
picks her way

from grave
to
grave

crossing

marbled
linoleum

stepping
on
cherubs

two women

walking in sync,
one with a chocolate lab,
the other, a violin case

the faint clatter
of penny-brown oak leaves

there are voices

in the wind tonight
I can't make them out

did you get the URL
I sent
for the wildflower seeds ?

a cup
of
gossip

and you're gone

motes in a slant
of sunlight

after
one glass
of wine

the spill

of a decade's
discontent

the red
tinge

of tail lights
on
the snow

of your leaving

the moon is cloud-fleeced
and wolves worry the forest

it's time

for dark chocolate
and
warm saké

for Joy

if some starless night
you appear beside my bed

in black

I'm sure
you'll take my breath
away

for ai li

a tapestry of dark forest

deer and owls stare out
with Rousseau eyes

how I'd love
to take you with me
into the warp & woof

the suck of mud and then we're across

this rainy a.m.

a splash
of forsythia

holds me
at my
study window

tree cathedral
& me ...

a church
of
one

all the beliefs

of east and west
at finger tip and tongue

and yet
the hundred acre wood of Pooh
is world enough

a hang glider
of sticks and newspaper

I knew
it wouldn't carry me
over field and woods

but still I drew the plans

lifeless

from
the asphalt's
heat

and
swept aside
by traffic

thousands
of monarchs
litter

the roadside

the river,

all
trickle
&
bone

the leaves
pant

each grape
a raisin

under a migraine
of clouds

her saffron umbrella
pops
into bloom

lilacs stir in the churchyard

at the sidewalk café
some 3 or 4 sparrows
gather at my feet –
you have crumbs
we have nooo crumbs

after wafers
and raspberry sherbet
we part under
pink blossomed crabapples
to go our separate ways

moonlight on the river
trolleys rattling in the distance

a night made for whispering

sweet nothings
in
italics

for a moment
under moon and
milky way

parallel worlds touch

the impossible heat
of her beach-tanned body

she rises

out of her warm scent
and in a single step

is clothed
in stained-glass
light

candied yams

the clatter of silverware
on bone china

the lingerie
her husband
will never see

a cottage, a stream
some cows
a boy and his dog

that's where I want to be

inside
the willowware

biting into an apple
warmed through by the sun

kicking a tin can

down
the
road

"come on you kids ...

wash between your fingers
don't forget your thumbs"

sand in her shoes
and the heat of the day
in her jeans

in his canvas swing

the baby's
infectious laughter –

my face ached
from so much
ear to ear

and I
only eleven years old,

so soon
so young to ache

fever broken,

the child
faintly smiles

fireflies
in
a mason jar

at dusk

the feral cat
leaping
at insects

brings
my boyhood

she tosses the stick
and tosses the stick

her bodice is loose & low

the dog and I
are easily made
glad

topless in jeans
she moves about the kitchen
beyond the window
a tree of yellow apples
bright in the late November fog

another scorcher

and the house
all to herself

a few
daring selfies –
why not ?

a dragonfly
hovers

then darts away

you surface among
the lily-pads
wet and smiling

how quiet the apples

and the trees
they live in

a small bird
dips
and disappears

standing

on the porch
listening

to the silence
of woods
and snow

the winter trees
are stuffed with fog

only the crunch
of my boots

in the cotton silence

fresh fallen snow

trying to match
the stride

of one
who went before

while

the world
falls apart

I coax the feral cat
to eat
from my hand

awake

we lie side by side
in the dark

pretending
to
sleep

at first light

the feral cat
is waiting for me
to fill his bowl

and what if I didn't wake
one morning ?

the horizon
that with me

always took
a step
ahead

now waits

let the day lily
be
my metaphor

let
the long day end

just so

dusk tightens

fruit bats take
to the air

holding hands
we lean our backs

against the warmth
of
the stone façade

at day's end

my world shrinks
to an infinite space

desklamp
paper
pen

no wine   no moon

still
I make my song

from this pool
of lamplight and the void
around me

◇

epilogue

funk & fugue
a tanka sequence

fen, fern & dusky forest
thinly layered sunlight . . .
gold-questing Norsemen
stomp
across my vision

what if?
in a jungle of jewelweed,
a patch-sized village
of tiny folk
brigadoons at my feet

look!
chalked on the rock face
a stickman & woman –
holding hands they spirit-float
over bracken

cool air
from a crevice in the rock –
I could squeeze through, but ...
but they'd be waiting,
funk & fugue

oily sunlight
through tendrils of jungly woods –
what if I stumble upon
an ancient temple,
a fearful prophecy?

<>

THUNDER AND APPLE BLOSSOMS

selected haiku

*

selected and edited by
Stanford M. Forrester / sekiro

dusk
and the daylily all but done

yellow leaves
at year's end

small griefs
haunt
my footsteps

on the cheek
of the brass
teapot

the embers'
cherry rouge

snow falling falling
   through a claw of apple boughs
   – my failing mother

over glazed snow a spider crawling toward the end
   of February

   again today

   I worked
   on the *big* poem –

   soon
   there will be
   crocuses

maternity ward –
mine
the only home-picked
wildflower bouquet

under a sky
by Monet,
the girl
in the strawberry dress

where the small lake
leaks away . . .
a tea-dark gurgle

midnight
say the prayer
take the pill

midnight
a whistler and his footsteps

if not
for the dripping
faucet –
alone
tonight

her number
not in my brain
but my finger

at the VFW
same scar
different story

in the brass
door knob
a distorted face

I grip
and twist

photo gallery
I've never seen eggs
look so nude

first the model gets naked
then nude

crossing the lawn barefoot
      arriving
            in dew time

weeping
she
embraces me

the brook's
small babble

cicada afternoon –

in
the sanctuary's
coolness

stained-glass
parables

      a screen door
      bangs –

      all past summers
      summarized

      in one brief
      report

Maple Street   my shady past

thunder and apple blossoms
her naked presence in the orchard grass

                              a bare midriff – that's all it takes

stuck
for an answer

I lower
my eyes –

her ten
red
toenails

evening settles
on the patio
a dusky lingerie
still warm

the restlessness of leaf shadows on a crimson couch

      her diary –
      if only I hadn't forced its tiny lock . . .

           she's been here
           and gone . . . the gift
           of her perfume

turning
from the window

her blouse
full of sunshine
and shadow

back home
willing to fix the argument
for sex

lust
over the kitchen table
a 60 watt bulb

pussywillows
behind
the Court House

the smart click
of high heels

              shaking
              the stone from
              her shoe

              a white opal
              swings

              from between
              brown breasts

        she loiters
           smelling a spray of violets
            – the nape of her neck

this inch-sized frog traveling a foot each   leap

stuck

on the blond curl
of the flypaper

a buzzing triad

in the sprinkler's rainbow
a wasp loses
        altitude

a snake released –
the feel of it
  stays in my hand . . .

first cicada
one long sizzling syllable says it's summer

watching the loggers work
I rub my paper cut

a dusting of snow
the chickadees's cluttered cuneiform

        our fingers
        touch
        the small
        arithmetic
        of coins

clasping my dad's hand
    as once he gripped his father's hand
        whose hand had once . . .

after his stroke
a safety razor –

      the strop still hangs
      by the door

      the
      little
      bird
      rides
      the
      tall
      weed
      down

late sunlight
    climbs the hotel wall
        cigarette by cigarette

    dear fly
    we can't go on like this

cruel words
the inadequacy of long-stemmed roses

a sudden
flush from peach
to rose

every branch
aglitter
with ice

on my palm
        this snowflake
                swiftly becoming . . .

Sidewalk Café

sidewalk café
I tell the dog
'don't even think about it'

crumbs crumbs crumbs
is there anything
not crumbs

having refused the dog
I feed the sparrow
                 – why?

a yellow jacket
circles my coffee mug
                 – I wait

crumpled napkin
the sparrow's slight crouch
before take-off

         * * *

Cat & I

cat pushes glass figurine
a little . . . & a little . . . & . . .
ok, I get up

cat & I pretend she's hidden

cat comes
to an accordion stop
it's raining

it's raining
cat tries the back door

cat & I watch rain at open door

kitten runs up my jeans
& over my shoulder
I spill some water

* * *

About the Author

Larry Kimmel was born in Johnstown, PA. He holds degrees from Oberlin Conservatory and Pittsburgh University, and has worked at everything from steel mills to libraries. He lives quietly in the hills of western Massachusetts.

To learn more about the work
of Larry Kimmel see:
https://larry-kimmel.com/

Other Books by Larry Kimmel

in an upstairs room

this hunger, tissue-thin

outer edges

the colors of ash

the horizon waits

Adrift: selections from Blue Night

thunder and apple blossoms: selected haiku

Collected Haiku: 1997 – 2017

Collected Poems and Prose 1968 - 2008

selected poems 1968 - 2022

a river years from here

Unworldly Wind

Whip-poor-will Hollow (novella)

(Collaborative Books)

Side by Side (tanka with Joy McCall)

Blue Smoke (cherita with sheila windsor)

sun-bourne rain (cherita with sheila windsor)

(Out-of-Print Books)

a spill of apples (with Carol Purington) (out-of-print)

Betrayal On Maple Street (out-of-print)

As Far As Thought Can Reach (out-of-print)

alone tonight (out-of-print)

Blue Night (out-of-print)

The Piercing Blue of Sirius: selected poems
1968 - 2008 (out-of-print)

Printed in Great Britain
by Amazon

32889630R00235